I AM A FUGITIVE FROM A
GEORGIA CHAIN GANG!

I AM A FUGITIVE FROM A GEORGIA CHAIN GANG!

Robert E. Burns

Quid Pro Books

New Orleans, Louisiana

I AM A FUGITIVE FROM A GEORGIA CHAIN GANG!

Originally published in 1932 by the Vanguard Press, New York, and The Macfadden Publications, Inc.

Published in 2017 by Quid Pro Books.

ISBN: 978-1-61027-376-3 (pbk.)
ISBN: 978-1-61027-377-0 (hbk.)
ISBN: 978-1-61027-374-9 (eBook)

QUID PRO BOOKS
Quid Pro, LLC
5860 Citrus Blvd., Suite D-101
New Orleans, Louisiana 70123
www.quidprobooks.com

qp

Publisher's Cataloging-in-Publication

Burns, Robert E. (Robert Elliott), 1892-1955.

 I am a fugitive from a Georgia chain gang! / Robert E. Burns.

  p. cm. — (Journeys & memoirs)

 Originally published: New York: Vanguard Press, 1932.

 1. Burns, Robert Elliott. 2. Criminals—Georgia—Biography. 3. Convict labor—Georgia. 4. Crimes and criminals—Georgia. I. Title. II. Series.

HV 6248.B79A3 2017   357.73'05—dc21

CONTENTS

Robert Elliott Burns (1892-1955)

FOREWORD

I AM a fugitive!

I am a fugitive from the law—but NOT FROM JUSTICE.

Discharged from the army, after the World War, a broken man, I committed a petty crime in Georgia, was caught, convicted, sentenced to ten years on the Georgia Chain Gang.

On June 21, 1922, after serving a few months, I made a miraculous escape. I went to Chicago. After seven years of honest and industrious toil I beat my way up from being an unknown escaped convict to holding an honored place in society. I was in love with a beautiful woman, who loved me also. Another woman, knowing my secret for years and using it to her advantage, betrayed me.

In the midst of a winning fight to defeat extradition, I voluntarily returned to the jurisdiction of Georgia, expecting to receive human understanding and common justice. I got neither.

A country-wide effort was made to secure my release. But it failed. The law demanded its pound of flesh.

On September 4, 1930, I made another successful escape from the chain gang.

I have just suffered from a catastrophe that would destroy the average man. I have escaped the bottomless depths of Hell.

But Georgia cannot win! Risking detection and a return to the chain gang, I have decided to write the true story, WHILE IN HIDING, of my entire case.

ROBERT E. BURNS

INTRODUCTION

By the Rev. Vincent G. Burns

UNDER A fiery Georgia sun. On a ribbon of red clay road. Glittering like an endless bronze snake among the trees. Throwing dust into your lungs. We are hiking on a broiling summer's day from the little town of La Grange, Georgia, to a point three miles southwest. To the Troup County convict camp, isolated among the cotton-clad hills of south Georgia.

The Negroes, lounging around their shacks on this hot Sunday afternoon, sit up to stare at the strangers. The shacks in which they live are one- or two-room buildings on stilts. Buildings that huddle together along the red clay road and house the families of the colored folks. Little absolutely naked babies toddle around the doors. Grandfathers and grandmothers sit silently on steps of houses. Not a single uplifting element surrounds these cottages, except the green of the trees and the blue of the skies.

On we go, down the road. We pass a bend. Hot and tired we sit down on a rock and survey before us the Troup County stockade. A level clay esplanade, blazing under the sun. A well-sweep. Beyond that a long, low, gray building. Windows barred. A black chimney in the back. Beyond that a stockade where one sees mules and wagons. A guard, heavily armed, sits talking with a trusty at the entrance. A few more trusties in stripes walk about the clay esplanade. Red dust on everything, trees, buildings, men.

We get up and go over to where the guard is sitting. He says to us "What do you want?" We tell him who we are. He sends the trusty inside. After a long wait the trusty comes out. "All right!" We follow him inside.

We find ourselves in a grim, gray, dungeon-like room. Through the chicken-wire and iron bars, where a number of convicts are talking to relatives, we see about seventy men. On the right-hand side of the room, huddled in little groups or pacing up and down in chains, we see about thirty or forty Negroes. On the left-hand side of the room are thirty or forty white men.

On a raised platform immediately in front we see several burly guards, with heavy six-shooters on their hips.

An intense, awful spell of silence seems to be gripping everything. The only sounds are the clanking of the chains and the whispering of the prisoners, as they converse with their friends.

A burly guard calls out shrilly in the silence, "Burns!"

Out from among the white convicts steps a slim, short figure.

He walks stooped over, as if each step were an effort. He is thin and emaciated. He lifts his eyes to see who it is, eyes full of suffering and dread, and yet with a degree of expectancy.

Suddenly a sob, half-choked, but distinctly audible, comes to his lips, "Mother!" He runs to the sad, gray-haired woman who stands behind the chicken wire. "Elliott, my boy!" she cries. They cannot embrace. They cannot even touch each other's hands. They look into each other's eyes. Neither can say a word. They stand looking at one another helplessly.

He turns to me. Tears are blinding his eyes. "For God's sake, Vince," he says, "why didn't you come sooner?"

Who was this man? Why was he here? What had he done?

This man was my own brother, and the gray-haired mother my own mother. This tragedy that was enacted before me was partly my own. The steps that led up to it were as I briefly relate them here.

When America declared war on the Central Powers in 1917 Robert E. Burns was a successful young accountant in New York City. He enlisted a few days after the declaration of war and arrived in France with a medical detachment of the 14th Railway Engineers in the summer of 1917. From September, 1917, until the armistice in November of 1918 he was almost constantly at the front. He served in Flanders and in the Chateau Thierry, Argonne and St. Mihiel drives. In the medical detachment he was required to attend the wounded and bury the dead. The strain was terrific during the heavy fighting.

When he returned from the war we were at once aware that something serious had happened to him. He was not wounded externally but he was mentally wounded—a casualty upon whose injury one could not place a finger, but a more deeply wounded casualty for that very reason. He was nervously unstrung and mentally erratic—a typical shell-shock case.

We tried to get him into a government rest camp but without his co-operation we were unable to establish the nature of his malady. Again we tried to get him work. But it was always the same story—he was too nervous to stay put long enough to fill a position of the simplest kind.

He grew more and more despondent and bitter with his fate. Finally he disappeared—wandered off in a fog of mental discouragement.

For three weeks we had no word whatever of his whereabouts. We had almost given him up for dead when one morning there came a letter from one John Echols, an attorney of Atlanta, Georgia, to the effect that Robert E. Burns of Brooklyn, N. Y., had been arrested and was being held without bail for trial in the Criminal Court in Atlanta.

We were amazed and shocked. We knew not what horrible crime he had committed. We were panicky. We got in touch with Echols, who promptly reported to us that my brother had been sentenced to from six to ten years in the chain gang.

For doing what? This is what had happened. Mr. Echols told us later that when my brother was arrested and brought into court he was actually barefooted and in rags. He had arrived in Atlanta in that condition after riding the freight cars from the North. He was penniless. He was in a state of mental breakdown. He had no friends, had never been in the South before. He went for food and shelter to the Salvation Army, where he met two strangers. He told them that he was looking for a job. They said they would get him one. Together they went to a grocery store on Pryor Street, Atlanta. There one of the two men told him he was going to help in a hold-up of the store. He refused, and started to walk away. One of the men pulled a gun and threatened to plug him if he made any attempt to get out of the robbery.

The store was held up and $5.80 was taken. The three men were later arrested, tried and sentenced. My brother was sentenced to from six to ten years in the chain gang for a crime he had no intention whatever of committing and during which he was a mental casualty as a result of his service in the World War.

My brother was first taken to the Fulton County chain gang but was later transferred to the Campbell County gang. He entered the chain gang shattered in body and mind. He should have been in a hospital rather than under the back-breaking conditions of the chain gang.

From the first the hard labor and poor food on the chain gang completely undermined his constitution. He was driving his poor war-shattered body with all his will-power in "keeping the lick", but as he was growing weaker and weaker, he resolved to escape at the first opportunity.

The opportunity came in a dramatic way. A Negro on the gang bent my brother's shackles with a sledge-hammer so he could slip out of his chains. When an opportune time came he escaped from the chains, left the gang, got into the bushes, eluded the dogs and made his way into Atlanta.

After his escape he went to Chicago. His first job there was in the stock yards. Later he secured a better position as accountant for a lumber company. Here he was able to save a little money, with which he embarked in the real-estate business. He was especially successful in renting and subleasing apartments.

He acquired a fair-sized bank account, and with this in 1924 he laid the foundation for *The Greater Chicago Magazine*. Against herculean handicaps, through heart-breaking reverses, working night and day and living from hand to mouth through months and years he managed eventually in 1929 to build this magazine into a place of importance in the business and real-estate circles of a great city. In May of that year he held a position of high public trust in the life of Chicago, and occupied a modern suite of offices in one of the finest buildings in Chicago.

Considering his rise from fugitive to business executive in a space of seven years, one must recognize in him those qualities of courage, perseverance, industry and honesty which lie close to the bed-rock of American life. He had lived down his past. Seven years before he was a convict fleeing from the chain gang, a shell-shock casualty of the war, a penniless, friendless vagabond in a great city. Now, his mental health fully recovered, he was respected and admired by the leading men of a great metropolis. Now he had created a business which was rapidly assuming a constructive and vital place in the progress of Chicago.

One morning two men stepped into his office. They opened their coats and displayed their badges. They told him they had come to arrest him and return him to Georgia. He had always lived under his own name. Unaided, Georgia would never have sought him in Chicago. Some one must have turned him in. Who was it?

When my brother first arrived in Chicago he had secured a room in a boarding house in south Chicago. The owner of this house was a woman named Mrs. Emily del Pino Pacheo, a Spanish divorcee. While my brother was living in this house, Mrs. Pacheo one day out of curiosity read a letter from my father to my brother, in which letter the Georgia experience was referred to. At this time Mrs. Pacheo was violently in love with my brother, although this affection was not reciprocated by him.

This woman, under the spell of what she thought was love, determined to marry my brother and threatened him with exposure if he failed to accede to her requests. Under fear of exposure he acceded to her demands and they were married. Their life together was not a happy one, and as my brother could not stand it any longer, he finally decided he would remove his residence to downtown Chicago.

In the early spring of 1929 my brother met a young woman by the name of Lillian Salo. She was a charming, cultured young woman and at once captured the heart of the now successful young magazine editor. Together they went to the legal wife of Robert E. Burns and begged her aid in getting a divorce. This she was perfectly willing to do, stating the terms of alimony and agreeing to secure a lawyer, whose fee was to be paid by my brother.

But at this time she took sick, was removed to the hospital and almost died. My brother paid her hospital bills of over one thousand dollars, and incidentally helped to save her life.

A few days after he had footed the hospital bills and a few weeks after the divorce proceedings had begun, detectives arrived in his office. His wife had turned him over to the Georgia authorities.

Our first inkling that the Georgia police were after my brother came in an indirect way. A Brooklyn detective called at the home of one of my relatives with a picture of Robert E. Burns, taken in Chicago, and asked my aunt several questions concerning his whereabouts. As soon as I learned that the man-hunt was on I sent a telegram to him at his South Chicago address. But he never received it. His wife intercepted it.

Word soon came of his arrest. I boarded the Twentieth Century Limited and rushed to Chicago.

Meanwhile my brother had secured bail of $5,000, put up by one of Chicago's leading business men. I found him in his offices, surrounded by many friends and in the midst of plans to fight extradition. He was dazed by the blow that had fallen.

The next day my brother, his attorneys and myself went to Springfield, Illinois, to plead with Governor Emmerson to prevent extradition. I was armed with a letter from my friend, Carl Sandburg, the poet, to a prominent citizen in Springfield. Through this citizen I was able to obtain an audience with the Governor. He was very sympathetic with my brother's case, and mentioned a dozen telegrams, including one from Jane Addams, which he had received from prominent men and women in Chicago. The Governor gave me the impression, although it was not explicitly stated, that he would not sign the extradition papers.

On the way back to Chicago we picked up a newspaper on the front page of which was a headline proclaiming a state of excitement in Georgia over the recapture of my brother. The newspaper reported that the Mayor of Atlanta recommended a pardon for my brother, that prominent citizens and even the State Legislature of Georgia were in favor of granting him a full reprieve.

Upon reading this article my brother remarked that if the attitude was as favorable as the newspaper reported he would go back to Georgia and get his pardon. He discussed the matter with his lawyers and decided to send Mr. Cameron Latter to Georgia to look the ground over. Mr. Latter went to Georgia and, on his return, reported that sentiment was favorable for a pardon and that he had secured William Schley Howard, the leading attorney of Atlanta, to represent my brother.

Also, at this time a number of remarkable editorials in leading news-papers of the larger cities had brought my brother's case into the eye of the entire country. His case became of national significance. Everyone was asking: What will the state of Georgia do? Can it be possible that the authorities will reincarcerate a man who has been a good citizen for seven years? Will this war veteran get a square deal from the prison people in Atlanta?

Meanwhile Mr. Vivian Stanley, a member of the Georgia Prison Commission, had arrived in Chicago. He appeared in Judge David's court during the habeas corpus proceedings and said that if Robert E. Burns would waive extradition, return to Georgia and pay the state the cost of his recapture, he would receive a pardon in a very short time. Upon talking the matter over with Judge Stanley my brother agreed to waive extradition, to abandon the habeas corpus proceedings and to return to Georgia, assured from all quarters that his pardon was only a matter of days.

My mission in Georgia was to plead my brother's case before the session of the Prison Commission at a hearing to be held early in August,

1929, at the state capital in Atlanta, Georgia. I came to Georgia with high hopes. The following points in his favor caused us to believe that a pardon or parole would be granted:

1. Judge Rainey, the chairman of the Prison Commission, had granted us the hearing in a personal letter to me.

2. Governor Hardman had written me saying my brother's case would be promptly passed upon in the light of human sympathy and understanding.

3. Our attorney, Mr. William Schley Howard, had informed Mr. Latter that in sixty days he would secure a pardon.

4. The State of Georgia, through a member of the Prison Commission, had promised in Chicago an early parole or pardon if my brother would waive extradition, which he had done, and return to Georgia.

5. The leading citizens of Georgia with whom I came in contact were unanimous in their opinion that he should be pardoned.

6. The ring-leader in the original crime had already been pardoned by the State of Georgia.

7. We felt that all the facts concerning my brother's case would recommend him for parole to any just prison board: the fact of his being a shell-shocked veteran of the war, the fact that he had taken part in the robbery under compulsion, and the fact that he had proved in Chicago his capacity to fill a useful, honest place in society.

We were to be rudely disappointed.

The hearing was held in a small room in the quarters of the Prison Commission on the second floor of the state capitol building in Atlanta.

Behind a long table sat the three Prison commissioners. Judge Rainey, a man with white, curly hair, an eye as cold as steel, a square jaw, with a facial expression that never changed. Judge Johns, a quiet, decorous man, baldheaded, even-tempered, a man who gave the impression of kindness. Judge Stanley, a tall, angular man, who stuttered slightly.

The room was filled with listeners, among them many newspaper men. Judge Rainey said: "All right, let's hear what you've got to say, and make it short, because we have many other cases to hear!"

William Schley Howard, John Echols and I were sitting at the table directly in front of the commissioners. Echols spoke first. He reviewed the case as he had known it from the beginning, and read a very sympathetic editorial from the *Atlanta Georgian*. Then I was called on. I made a sincere plea for my brother, reviewing the history of his case from childhood up.

William Schley Howard then made a brilliant appeal for justice and fair-dealing. His arguments were cogent and persuasive and impressive. But as I watched the faces of the commissioners my heart sank. They were as hard and cold as a dungeon wall. Not a flicker of sympathy. Not a trace of anything but stolid indifference. I was convinced then that they had already made up their minds.

A man by the name of Stephens then arose. He had been sitting in a corner unnoticed. We learned later that Judge Rainey had summoned him to attend the hearing. Stephens was assistant Solicitor in Fulton County, Georgia, a slim, very short person with thick eye-glasses, but eyes like a hawk. He introduced into the hearing a despatch from my brother's wife filled with the most lurid accusations against him. He said: "This man is a convict. He belongs in the chain gang. He is a habitual criminal. He has violated the laws of Georgia and owes Georgia a debt. We intend to collect that debt and we expect to keep this thief in the chain gang until it is collected!"

I arose to my feet. I begged for the right to answer the accusations which had been made against my brother. Judge Rainey waved his hand and declared the hearing closed.

This hearing occurred in August, 1929. No word came to us concerning the result of our plea. In September I was visiting my mother in Pittsfield, Massachusetts. One day my mother screamed. We rushed in to see what was the matter. Before her on the floor was a local newspaper and on the front page a news item with a statement that the petition of Robert E. Burns for pardon had been denied by the Georgia Prison Commission. My mother was hysterical for twenty-four hours. We could do nothing with her. She had felt sure my brother would be pardoned and this disappointment left her completely crushed.

Might I add, just here, that this cruel torture which Georgia has so unjustly laid upon my brother has resulted not only in the shattering of my brother's life, but was one of the contributing causes of my father's death, an element in the death of my wife's father, and the cause of my mother's poor health, which she has suffered ever since the first news came out of Georgia in 1922.

After we collected our thoughts following the shock received from the disappointing news, we, my mother and I, decided to go to Georgia to place our plea personally before Governor Hardman. In Georgia the Governor has the right of pardon and may exercise it independently of the Prison Commission.

We rushed to Georgia, arriving there on Labor Day morning. When we inquired at the Governor's office we learned he was at his summer home in the country. At first we thought we might make the trip to see him there, but we changed our minds and made an appointment to see him the following week when he would be in his office.

When the time came we had with us William Schley Howard, our attorney, and three of the leading ministers of Atlanta.

Our three friends, the ministers, were sympathetic with the human appeal for justice in my brother's case. They pleaded for his pardon. Occasionally the Governor would interrupt with some slight objection. But on the whole he seemed to be in a mood of sympathy. Mother made a plea for my brother, stressing his weak physical condition. Then I said a few words.

The Governor sat silent for a moment. Then he said: "I do not think a man could be a criminal with a mother like you. I believe Burns should have another chance. I will tell you what I propose to do. I will look up his physical condition at the time he entered the war service. I will have him examined physically now, and if I find him in worse physical condition now than at the time he entered the service I will take steps towards his parole."

We have never heard from that day to this a single word from the Governor as to whether he made an examination or instituted the investigation or took steps toward the parole as he promised to do that day in his office in the capitol building in Atlanta.

We were grabbing at straws. So next we paid a visit to the office of the solicitor-general in Atlanta, John A. Boykin. This office is on the third floor of the Criminal Courts Building in Atlanta.

After waiting a full hour, Stephens, the assistant solicitor, came out and stopped in front of my mother.

"Could you kindly get us an audience with Mr. Boykin?" said my mother.

"Who are you?" was the gruff retort.

"I am the mother of Robert E. Burns," she replied. "I have come all the way to Atlanta to try to see the men who can grant him a pardon."

"Well, I want to tell you," said Stephens, shaking his fist in my mother's face, "I want to tell you that any damn Yankee who comes down here to steal is going to get all that's coming to him!"

With that he walked away and left us sitting there, wondering where on earth all the Southern chivalry and hospitality we had heard so much about could be.

I then went up to one of the clerks in the office and demanded to see Mr. Boykin. I was ushered into a close, stuffy office. A desk stood in the center of the room. Over the desk crouched a man whose head was almost clean-shaven, whose back was broad and who gave the appearance of being a person of great height. But when he rose he stood crouched over in the attitude of one who is ready to spring. He turned toward me a face in which there was no trace of kindness. This was John A. Boykin, the most feared man in the state of Georgia.

He waved me to a chair. I told him I came to ask his help in securing a pardon for my brother. He fixed me with a cold gray eye. "Your brother is a criminal," he said. "We have given him the sentence that he deserves, for highway robbery. Sentiment has nothing to do with it. We are going to give him what he deserves as a menace to society. Good day!"

And John Boykin swung around in his swivel chair, and I walked from that office with a chilled and aching heart.

My mother decided to remain in Georgia to be near my brother, still hoping that the Governor would keep his promise. I went to Washington with the hope that the President and the federal government would see the justice of my brother's case and pave the way for his pardon. This hope was to be shattered. I laid my brother's case before Senators and Representatives, before General Hines of the Veterans Bureau and Mr. Ralph L. Chambers of the Disabled American Veterans, but nothing was accomplished.

Weeks and weeks went by. Slowly hope seemed slipping away. My mother's letters grew more and more desperate. She was cracking under the terrific strain in Georgia. One who has not passed through an experience of this kind cannot understand it. To have a son in trouble is bad enough, to have to wait in suspense without hope is worse, but to have the strain of dealing with hostile officials is all but fatal.

Mother finally returned North. She reported that Judge Rainey had told her the Prison Commission had a rule that a man cannot petition for pardon until he has been in the gang at least twelve months. Why, then, had he let us come all the way to Georgia for a hearing in August? Why had he not told us in the first place we would have to wait twelve months? Why did not Judge Stanley explain this to my brother in Chicago, when instead he promised him a pardon in sixty days?

We swallowed this bitter pill and determined to concentrate on a final drive for a pardon the following summer.

Mother went to Chicago and interviewed hundreds of people there for affidavits in my brother's behalf. I went again to Washington. Also I secured affidavits from old friends who knew my brother from childhood and incidentally sought help from a number of prominent citizens of both North and South.

Our effort to get justice for Robert E. Burns cost our family five thousand dollars and innumerable trips all over the country. I myself made two trips to Chicago, three trips to Atlanta, two trips to Washington, D. C., two trips to Trenton, N. J., one trip to Savannah, Ga., one trip to Raleigh, N. C., uncountable trips to La Grange, Ga., from Atlanta, and many, many calls on persons in New York and New Jersey.

Among the persons to whom I personally appealed were the following: Calvin Coolidge, Clarence Darrow, Jane Addams, Joab H. Banton, Judge Mackay of Hackensack, N. J., Judge Crain of New York City, Carl Sandburg, George Gordon Battle, Robert Tyre Jones, Jr., Paul Hutchinson of the *Christian Century*, Robert Morss Lovett, Harry Emerson Fosdick, Josephus Daniels, Ambassador Walter E. Edge, Asst. Postmaster General Irving Glover, General Hines, Hunt Chipley of Atlanta, Preston Arkwright, President of the Georgia Power Company, Representatives Perkins, Black, Fort, Ramspeck and Tilson, Senators Harris and George of Georgia, Senator Royal S. Copeland of New York and Senator Borah of Idaho. Also the following Governors: Emmerson of Illinois, Larson of New Jersey, Roosevelt of New York and Hardman of Georgia.

Many of these friends were very cordial and kind to me. They tried their level best to be of help and almost unanimously they were openly friendly to my brother's case.

But in my travels I had a chance to look behind the stage at the machinery of government. And, especially with reference to Georgia, this is what I found:

1. Most officials were tangled up in red tape like flies in fly-paper.

2. The machinery of law was a brutal thing, designed to destroy and not to save.

3. The treadmill of tradition and custom had so paralyzed the minds and hearts of officials that they were no longer able to discriminate humanly as to plain justice.

The twelve months of probation were nearly up. Judge Rainey had promised that if we would wait twelve months and if my brother's conduct as a prisoner during that time was good a pardon would only be a matter of routine. The hearing was granted for the first week of July, 1930.

Mother left for Georgia in June. I arrived the first of July with five sets of affidavits, each one of which contained eighty-six affidavits of leading citizens of Chicago certifying to my brother's good character, letters and affidavits from old friends of my brother, an affidavit of the minister who baptized him, and a number of papers concerning his war record, etc. These we filed with the Prison Commission. In addition I had enlisted the aid of some powerful friends who were prepared to bring some real pressure to bear on the Prison Commission. It looked as though we could not lose.

Meanwhile my brother labored in the chain gang. Drove his broken body by sheer power of will to endure the brutal toil of the Georgia roads.

While I am speaking of this I might as well add a few more words which show my brother's plight in its true light. In recent years Governor Hardman commuted the sentences of two convicted embezzlers, who had stolen thousands of dollars from the public. He refused to parole or pardon my brother, despite the facts aforementioned: his war service, his unwillingness to take part in the crime, his seven years of upright life in Chicago.

Also, in this connection, a recent news item from Virginia is of interest:

CONVICT, BACK, TO GO FREE

Richmond, Va., June 25—Governor Pollard said today he would pardon Jesse Straudeman, who voluntarily returned to the Virginia penitentiary on Monday after living the life of a good citizen in Youngstown, Ohio, since he escaped from a prison camp in 1916.

Here was almost an exact parallel to my brother's case. My brother voluntarily returned to Georgia and he had lived the life of a good citizen in Chicago. In addition he was a shell-shocked veteran of the war and had no desire to commit any crime.

Another case exactly parallel to my brother's occurred at the very time when he was put back in the chain gang in July, 1929. A man sentenced to from four to ten years in Mississippi escaped after three months. He went to Tulsa, Oklahoma, and became a railroad engineer. He was discovered and arrested. He sent a plea to the Governor of Mississippi asking for a pardon, and explained that if he was forced to abandon his work he would lose seniority rights. The governor of Mississippi pardoned him while he was still at his work in Oklahoma.

Another similar case was that of Frank Preston, who was arrested at St. Louis, Missouri, on a tip given in an anonymous letter. He had escaped from the Ohio penitentiary several years before. When Governor White of Ohio learned that Preston had been leading a respectable life as a restaurant manager, he pardoned him and returned him to his family.

All tolerant, humane Governors accept this as a precedent. It has happened hundreds of times and in every state in the union. Yet my brother, who had every point in his favor, not only his good citizenship in Chicago, but also his war service, his shattered condition at the time of the crime, his unwillingness to commit any crime, was returned and not only not pardoned but incarcerated in the worst chain gang camp in the state— the one at Troup County.

Why? I think I know the answer. At the time of his arrest in Chicago he condemned the chain gang system and told newspaper men of its brutalities. Because he had the courage to tell the truth the officials of Georgia determined to make an example of him. To punish him, in other words, for revealing the disgraceful prison system of Georgia.

Finally the day of our second hearing came. A furiously hot July morning. This time only Judge Rainey and Judge Johns are present. They sit in their shirt-sleeves behind the long table. The same uninterested boredom in their faces. The same cold, chilly reception.

William Schley Howard and I alone are there. Another case preceded ours. A poor hunch-backed old father is pleading for his son. It seems the boy was driving down the road and a child ran in front of his car and was killed. For this the boy got fifteen years in the gang. He has already served five. And now the poor broken-down father is pleading for his son. He needs him on the little farm. He can no longer do the work himself.

But the two judges who sit behind the table give no sign of leniency. The heart-breaking plea of this poor southern farmer would find response in any other court on earth.

My heart sinks again. What hope have we for kindness? Men who have hardened their hearts and closed their minds no longer are able to mete out plain justice.

Our case is called. Mr. Howard again presents a masterly argument for Robert E. Burns. Again the judges listen half-heartedly to the testimony. This is old stuff to them now. They know all about Robert E. Burns. But they go through the motions of a hearing. It is almost too obvious that they will merely file the case among a thousand others and do absolutely nothing about it.

That is exactly what happened. I had to leave Georgia shortly after the hearing. Mother stayed on and waited with the everlasting faith of a mother's heart, waiting and hoping against hope.

Finally she could no longer stand it. She went to Judge Rainey's office to ask for word. She there collapsed from sheer exhaustion and despair.

It was now September. Mother had returned from Georgia and we were visiting her at her home in Pittsfield. More than, two months had elapsed since the day of the hearing but no word had been received by any of us as to the Prison Commission's decision.

One evening, almost exactly a year to the day since we had heard the Commission's first adverse decision, I returned to find mother in violent hysterics. The news in the paper was not that his petition had been turned down, *but that he had escaped from the chain gang, for the second time.*

To me this was good news. But to mother and the other members of our family it was bad news. They were afraid he would be killed in the man-hunt or at the best be recaptured and reincarcerated for his full term of six to ten years, with a good chance also that he would suffer grave mistreatment at the hands of warden and guards.

The newspaper said that he simply walked away from the gang on the road when sent for a pail of water. But we knew something of his plan to escape, and it was a clever and daring plan.

One Sunday afternoon, at the time of the second hearing, my mother and I were visiting my brother at the Troup County stockade. We assured my brother that his pardon was certain. But he thought otherwise, and was deeply depressed. He said, "I want you to get a loan on my veteran's compensation." We asked why. "Because," he replied, "if the commission turns me down again I am going to escape." We urged him not to be foolish, to wait and trust in the good-heartedness of the commissioners. But no, he was determined. I secured the loan for him and he told us he would use it in breaking from the gang. I said to him, "Well, I don't like the chances you are taking, but if you do get away, come to Jersey. There is a state where I think we can get justice for you."

We found out later that he used the money to employ a local Georgian near the stockade to pick him up on an appointed morning in his car and take him to Atlanta.

When the morning arrived he broke from the gang, made the farmer's waiting car in a hail of bullets, rode hidden in the rumble seat seventy miles to Atlanta, where he changed his prison garb in a cheap clothing store, boarded a bus for Chattanooga, eluding two sheriffs who were watching for him in Rome, Georgia, and got safely out of Dixie in as hair-raising a flight as one can read in the most lurid fiction.

He had beaten them again—and single-handed.

What sane man or woman, knowing his heart-breaking story, will condemn him for his daring escape from a living hell? Who will not rather say that Robert E. Burns has proved himself a man of courage who has a soldier's right to a lawful place in society? Who will say that he would have done better under the same conditions?

After my brother's escape he decided to tell his story and publish it, with the hope that country-wide sentiment might be aroused in his behalf and that the Georgia chain gang might receive the national airing it deserved.

He wrote a serial story for the *True Detective Mysteries* magazine, which ran from January to June, 1931. This story exploded like dynamite in Georgia and reverberated from one end of the state to the other. It brought forth excited rejoinders from several members of the Prison Commission, who were obviously embarrassed by the revelations of chain gang life which it contained. Warden Hardy of the Troup County gang attempted to deny the charges brought by my brother regarding filth, brutality and overwork in the chain gang. But he was promptly contradicted by the *Macon, (Ga.) Telegraph*, on which paper a star reporter had been employed to investigate the chain gang system and to give a frank report on the truth or falsity of my brother's story.

Here is what the *Telegraph* said:

"The indictment Robert Elliott Burns has made in print of the Georgia penitentiary system is no stronger than the indictment made by Messers. Allen, Pilcher, Wall, Powell, Rivers and others of the state senate and house of representatives. There is a great deal of truth in what Burns has to say about conditions in Georgia prison camps. Not only is the observation drawn from checking up on the Burns story and from personal examination that basically the condition under which convicts are handled in these camps is a hell on earth, but it is abundantly supported by the written declaration of collective members of the Georgia general assembly."

In commenting on the attitude of the Prison Commission the *Macon Telegraph* went on to say:

"In dealing with matters of prison conditions and prisoners the office of the state prison commission is not a good place to expect to get cordial information. There is overmuch of the atmosphere of belief on the part of the commission that anything pertaining to information for the public touching operation of Georgia's penal institutions is none of the public's business. Where the matter sought has in it anything of a specifically enlightening or intimate nature the cork-screw process has to be applied to get anywhere."

Quite true. And it should be a very powerful corkscrew, or one will get absolutely nowhere, as we consistently found out.

The prison masters of Georgia were certainly dumbfounded by my brother's sensational escape and his devastating expose of the rotten conditions of the chain gang, which had received nation-wide circulation. Moreover, the storm of controversy which set in Georgia and ended with legislative action against the chain gang, maddened them still more. The prison commissioners came forward with violent attacks on Robert E. Burns. The warden of the Troup County chain gang openly stated that when he again gets his hands on my brother he will give him the "works"—

in other words, the brutal punishments of the sweat-box, the stocks and the double chains.

We soon realized that the enraged Georgia prison people were determined to recapture my brother. Our first intimation of a systematic search came one evening when a neighbor of ours called on the telephone and said that a strange man was standing on the sidewalk in front of our house and spying on us. I went out to see but he had disappeared. The neighbor said he had been standing there fully fifteen minutes. Exactly one week from that time, on the following Friday, I was coming home about 9 o'clock when suddenly a man appeared out of the bushes near my house and disappeared down the street. He had evidently been watching our home from a hiding-place nearby. The following week on the same night we noticed a man walking up and down in front of the house and watching our door. There was little doubt that this strange interloper was a Georgia spy. The Georgia people believed they would find my brother in or near my home.

Further developments followed. Through secret channels I learned that in the local post-office in Palisade, New Jersey, my mail was being watched and a transcript of all incoming mails made. A little later a department of justice man from the South appeared in our little town. He carried a picture of my brother and was attempting to trace him or locate him near my home. It was interesting to know that a federal official was being employed to run down my brother. When we were trying to get him a pardon we were told on many different occasions that his case was purely a state matter and that no federal aid could be given. The U. S. government evidently is willing to lend its aid to help in the destruction of a man but unwilling to aid in the attempt to work out his salvation.

Georgia will have a hard time finding Robert E. Burns this time. I am frank to say that I know where my brother is. He is physically and mentally in better condition than he has been since the war. He is employed in an honorable and useful position. We intend to exert every effort to restore him again to his rightful place in society.

My brother will never go back to Georgia. Were he captured again he would die rather than go again into the chain gang. But we still hope another door may open. No matter what happens we intend to fight his case to a finish.

In closing, let me say this.

Not only does this story possess the marvelous human interest of a first-hand prison document, but it is also a striking proof of the power of a human soul to rise triumphant in the face of gross injustice and primitive cruelty. Robert E. Burns spent eighteen heart-breaking months in the Georgia chain gang under conditions as harsh as any Jean Valjean or Toussaint L'Ouverture ever suffered. But he did not permit these untoward circumstances to weaken his mind or break his will, although they did almost destroy his body.

Before his commitment to the chain gang, a shell-shocked victim of the World War, it would have been easy, had he given way for an instant, for insanity to take possession of him. Instead, he struggled bravely against the wholly destructive conditions in which he found himself. Society, the very society which he had fought for in the war, in the war which injured his mind and shocked his nerve centers and left him a casualty, this society tried to destroy him. But it failed. It was one man's will against a world of blind injustice. And the one man won. Won his way back to sanity and freedom, though he had to escape twice to do it.

If people will only read his story with sympathetic understanding and pass it on for others to read there inevitably will be a wave of great indignation against this most inhuman, most un-American system—the chain gang. The public, once vividly conscious of the horrors and brutalities of chain-gang life, will rise in its wrath and force a clean-up.

The publication of my brother's story has already resulted in official action in Georgia to clean up conditions in the chain gangs. I believe also, partly as a result of his story, the State Legislature of Georgia is preparing to pass a bill abolishing the chain gang altogether, and substituting a saner, juster prison system.

My brother may be a fugitive. But he is the wholly innocent party in all that has transpired. He has been grossly injured. But he himself has injured no human soul. He fought, as he thought, for freedom in France, for the good of his country. His country has rewarded him with indifference in his need, with flagrant neglect, with outright injustice. His country has branded him a convict, and made him a hunted thing on the earth. His country, for which he suffered the tortures of hell in the Great War, has laid upon his heart the bitter burden of thanklessness.

But his spirit is not broken. Through it all he has come out braver and stronger—though deeply scarred with the lash of ingratitude and injustice.

Perhaps the time may come when the agonized prayers of a mother's heart will be answered, and the young soldier, whose tragic experiences date from the day he enlisted in the World War to fight in France, may be pardoned and again be a free man in his own land.

I AM A FUGITIVE FROM A GEORGIA CHAIN GANG!

CHAPTER I

The War Makes a Wanderer

"THERE GOES the bugle, Howard, blowing for the last assembly we'll stand 'til the next war!" said I.

"Gee whiz! won't it be great to get back in civies again, eh?—and oh, boy, I'm glad it's over; and now for the good times and the fine things we were promised over there," said Howard.

It was a beautiful day in May, 1919, at Camp Devens, Mass., where this conversation took place, the day when the famous 14th Engineers were being mustered out of service. This regiment had actually seen fifteen months of front-line warfare—going into action on the Somme front in August, 1917—and was still at the front in the Meuse-Argonne sector when the Armistice came on November 11, 1918.

One by one we passed through the little wooden hut—gave our last salute—drew our $60 bonus and all or any other money we had coming—signed the roll, received our discharges, and said our last goodbyes.

I drew altogether about $300, walked out of the cantonment, and was a free agent once more—free from the discipline of military restraint. My, how good it was to be alive—to be back in the good old U. S. A.—still whole and young, with life before me!

Before I left, I was in love with a beautiful girl in my own neighborhood. At our parting she promised to wait for me. But alas, upon my return home, I discovered she had married a war-time officer with a "Sam Browne" belt.

I guess it was the "Sam Browne" belt she fell for, and not the man in it, for they separated in a year or so.

I had dreamed of a happy home with this young lady as my wife—those dreams all soldiers have when lying in the mud and muck of trenches, ducking "Fritzies," "whiz-bangs," and "potato mashers," and machine-gun bullets.

The loss of the lady, however, was only the first shock I was to receive. For when the $300 was gone, I found that being an ex-service man was no recommendation for a position—rather it was a handicap.

The promises of the Y. M. C. A. secretaries and all the other "fountain-pen soldiers" who promised us so much in the name of the nation and the Government just before we'd go into action turned out to be the bunk. Just a lot of plain applesauce!

Really an ex-soldier with A. E. F. service was looked upon as a sucker. The wise guys stayed home—landed the good jobs—or grew rich on war contracts, making buttons or some other *essential* war necessity.

In trying to find a position in society and earn a decent, honest living, I found that ex-soldiers were a drug on the market. The position I left at $50 a week was filled. But I could get a job at $.40 per hour—$17.60 a week.

And I thought of a few of my buddies, dead, forgotten, pushing up poppies and with nothing but a little white cross to mark the spot somewhere in France, and thought, "No seventeen-sixty-a-week job for me. Is this how my country rewards its volunteers—the men who were ready and willing to sacrifice life itself that democracy might not perish? By coming out victorious we made this the richest nation on earth, and now, when it is all settled, we, who after all the ballyhoo is over, should get the most of our victory—we find we're only suckers, and get handed an existence instead of a competence.

"Well," said I, "it doesn't go for me. If I can't get what *I know* I deserve, I'll take nothing."

I went through hell for my country and my reward was the loss of my sweetheart and my position.

And so, I became a hobo—just drifting along and around—here, there, anywhere—watching the world pass by, without taking any really active part in its march across the pages of time.

The year 1922. The scene—Atlanta, Georgia. It is February, and a heavy, dismal sleet has been falling for two days. I am sitting in the lobby of a fifty-cent flop house—broke, weary, disgusted with life, sitting all alone by a wood fire in a tin stove.

Two men come in. They warm themselves by the stove.

"How's it going, buddy?" says the older of the two.

"Rotten," I reply.

"You're a stranger here," says he.

"Yeah."

"Where do you hail from?" he questions.

"New York," I answer.

"Do you want to make some easy money?"

"Well, I guess so, I'm as free from money as a turtle is from feathers. What is it?" I retort.

"I can't tell you now, but meet me right here at 8 A.M. tomorrow morning, and I'll show you how it's done," he comes back.

"I can't promise, because I'm flat broke, and so don't know where I'll be tonight—much less tomorrow morning," I tell him.

"Well, I'll tell you what I'll do. I need you in on this deal, and it means a couple of hundred dollars each, so I'll give you a dollar to keep you going until 8 A.M. tomorrow." And with this he pulls out a dollar and hands it to me.

I accepted it with thanks. Being broke, it was doubly welcome.

All this time the younger of the two stood by dumbly, never opening his mouth.

After handing me the dollar, the speaker turned to his partner, the dumb one, and said, "Come on, Moore, let's go."

And as a parting to me on the way out: "See you at eight tomorrow."

This all happened more quickly than it takes to read it—and I was left by the fire with a much-needed dollar bill.

I wondered what it was all about, but dismissed the whole thing until the next day. A hot beef stew, dry socks, and some cigarettes *now,* and let tomorrow take care of itself.

In the afternoon I had already forgotten about my early companions, and, with a full stomach and feeling better, I went out to the "East Point" railroad yards to catch a freight to New Orleans. The "Mardi Gras" was going on there, and I had a desire to see this spectacle. I made a freight all right and was started on the way, but a railroad bull saw me and also made the same train, and started coming over the tops toward me.

It was either get off or be pulled off and arrested for train riding. I jumped off, climbed over a wire fence, and got on the public highway. The bull came over as far as the fence and told me to stay on the highway, as he'd arrest me if he saw me on the railroad property again.

Alas!—what strange tricks Destiny and Circumstance play on the human race. If that bull had been somewhere else at that moment, I would have gone to New Orleans, and the entire course of my life would have been altered. And I would not be writing this story now.

CHAPTER II

The Wanderer Gets Into a Jam

NEXT MORNING broke fine and clear and warm. While I was washing in the crude basin (the place had no sinks), in come the two strangers of yesterday.

We all went out to eat breakfast, and I learned that the older man's name was Flagg and that he was an Australian and also fought in the war with the Aussies (the Australian troops in the British Army). The silent one, Moore, was a native of Georgia, and too young to have been in the war.

During breakfast, Flagg and I discussed war experiences and never once touched on the proposition of the "easy money."

After breakfast, Flagg lead the way toward the suburbs of Atlanta, out on Pryor Street, East.

When we were on the outskirts of Atlanta, Flagg stopped.

All the way out I kept quizzing him as to what his proposition was, but he carefully concealed his plans. Moore as usual remained silent.

It was about 9 A.M. when we halted at Flagg's request. While standing on Pryor Street, East, Flagg said to me, "Do you see that store over there?" pointing to a little cross-road grocery store.

"Sure," said I.

"Well," said Flagg, "the owner of that store is a Jew and he pays his bills in cash, and I know he has about a thousand dollars with him, as he is going to pay his bills today. We three are going to rob him and get that thousand dollars. I have a gun here and I will 'throw the cabbage' in his face and cover him while Moore goes to the cash register and you search his person for the roll."

I looked at Flagg in speechless amazement. I had expected anything but this. Such a proposition out of a clear sky took my breath away.

"Why, you could buy the whole store for two hundred and fifty dollars," I answered. "That place won't take in a thousand dollars in six

5

months—and besides, committing such a crime and taking such a chance—count me out."

"You are afraid, eh? You haven't got the guts, that's it. You're yellow!" Flagg came back at me.

And there we were; Flagg, Moore, and I, arguing on East Pryor Street, at 9 o'clock in the morning—me trying to find a way out, and Flagg insisting I go through with it. Finally I decided to go; leave them and go my own way.

At this, Flagg remarked, "You see that man talking to that woman on the porch across the street? Well, they have seen us all together, and while you are walking away Moore and I are going in and pull the job. Those two people will see you walking down the street, and as they have already seen you with us, they will connect you with the job, and whether or not you are in with us, you'll have to stand the gaff just the same, and get none of the dough."

I looked across the street and there was a salesman of some kind talking to a woman on the porch. The little grocery store was not fifty feet away, and I could picture myself trying to explain my awkward position of standing and talking with two robbers five minutes before they pulled a job. Try and get the cops or anyone else to believe you were not in on the racket—even if, as in my case, it was so.

While I was reflecting on the jam I was in and wondering if there was a way out, Flagg interrupted my thoughts with this crack: "And say, don't go pulling any tricks or try to make any squawk, see? I got the rod in my pocket and I'll plug you if you try anything funny, see?"

I saw I was in a hot spot. My morale had not been strengthened by my war experiences or my treatment when I got back to the U. S. A. I hadn't anything much to live for, anyway—and now, either decision I made would not clear me. I might just as well be shot for a goose or a gander. Flagg won; and the Burns that was, lost.

We went into the store. Flagg covered the proprietor with his gun—Moore got to the cash register but couldn't open it. In a trance I walked toward the proprietor, who now had his hands above his head. Somehow I got through the process of feeling his pants pockets for the supposed roll. I was like one in a dream. I couldn't find a thing, and there I stood, between Flagg and the owner, right in the line of fire, should Flagg pull the trigger. Something made me look into the face of that man standing in front of me with his hands above his head. What I saw in his eyes brought me to my senses in a flash. That one look and I was myself again.

In an instant I jumped aside and behind him, just as he was lowering his right hand a little. There in his right back hip pocket was a revolver with the butt sticking out. My hand was almost as quick as my eye, and I got his gun.

But now I was through. I refused to search him any more and all I wanted was to get away. Neither Moore nor I had ever been through such an experience before, and we acted like the amateurs we were. Flagg was the only calm and cool one of the four, and on the way out pulled the transmitter of the phone off the wall.

Moore got $5.80 out of the register.

Twenty minutes later Flagg, Moore and myself were all arrested and locked up in the police station.

After the police got through their investigations, they brought some twenty victims of recent robberies to look us over. All of them identified Flagg, but none identified either Moore or myself.

Flagg was indicted on twenty-one counts; Moore and I on one count. But the police tried their best to hook us up with some of Flagg's recent jobs. None of the victims could positively identify us, however, so the police were left with their suspicions, and had to be satisfied with the one charge against Moore and myself.

Flagg was tried first, pleaded guilty and asked for the mercy of the court. Judge Thomas of Valadosta was sitting in Fulton Superior Court hearing the case. He sentenced Flagg to from ten to fifteen years on two counts to run consecutively, twenty to thirty years in all.

Moore came next, pleaded guilty, asking for the mercy of the Court, and mentioned this as his first offense. He got from eight to twelve years.

I came last, pleading guilty, and asking the Court if I could say a few words before sentence was passed. The Court granted my request. I made an earnest plea—stating the facts as heretofore related—called attention to my mental attitude caused by the results of my treatment by society after my discharge from the war service—also that this was my first and last attempt at crime, and that this crime was committed through environment and not by direct intention. I pleaded for a minimum sentence. I got from six to ten years at hard labor.

Four days later I was on my way to the State Penitentiary of Georgia.

CHAPTER III

An Introduction to the Georgia Chain Gang

A ND HERE another surprise awaited me. I had never seen a penitentiary, but had read that they are large institutions of stone and are surrounded by a huge wall.

After about one hour's ride, we arrived at the so-called penitentiary. It was a place called Bellwood in Fulton County, Georgia. It consisted of a few old dilapidated low wooden buildings. Here I was put into a suit of "stripes"—no underwear or socks—just a two-piece suit of cotton "stripes," and given a pair of large brogans about four sizes too big for me.

Next I went to the blacksmith's shop. A heavy steel shackle was riveted on each ankle, and a heavy chain (similar to a trace chain) was permanently fixed to connect the shackles. There were thirteen links in the chain—making it impossible to take a full step. This was known as the "strad" chain.

In the middle of the chain (which ran from ankle to ankle) another chain was fixed. This chain was three feet long and on the end was an iron ring about as big as a silver dollar. This was called the upright chain.

In order to walk it was necessary to hold this last chain in your hand, to keep it from trailing on the ground.

When I had been properly chained and examined by one of the guards I was hustled into a truck and taken to Sandy Springs camp, also in Fulton County.

This was a long wooden building, one story high, with cots and mattresses along each side. The inside was just rough boards with an iron-barred window here and there, and open toilets down the center. At one end of this building was the mess hall, and at the other end, the washroom.

At night, another long chain was run down alongside of each cot. The prisoner had to sit on the cot and hold the iron ring of the upright chain in his hand while the guard ran this chain through the iron ring. This was called the building chain and was securely fastened at each end of the building after being run through the iron ring of each prisoner's upright chain.

Thus each prisoner was securely chained up each night and could only move three feet from his cot. Any movement of the prisoner caused the chains to rattle and a corresponding curse from the guard. If it was necessary to get up to use the toilets, the prisoner must first yell "Getting up" and then wait for the guard's reply "Get up." The whole process was very noisy and was accompanied by the clanking of heavy chains.

The chains the prisoners wore were permanently riveted on them, and were worn every minute of the time. They worked in them, slept in them, were a part of them. The chains could not be taken off unless they were cut off with a hammer and a cold chisel.

A leather contrivance (something on the style of a garter), called "leg belts" was attached to each leg to hold up the shackle and keep the strad chain off the ground, while working. The upright chain was looped through the belt and it also helped to keep the "strad chain" from tripping up the prisoner. The whole weighed about twenty pounds, and was exceedingly awkward and at times painful. Sometimes the shackles would rub sores on the ankles and this was known as "shackle poison."

We were awakened every morning at 3:30 A.M. by the process of a guard pulling the building chain through the iron ring of our upright—and if we did not get up and get a strong hold on the iron ring, we would find ourselves pulled out of bed and dragged to the next cot by our feet.

Very few of the prisoners removed their pants at night, preferring to sleep in them, rather than go through the Houdini trick of removing them through the shackles, which was a difficult task.

Breakfast was eaten by lamp light, and consisted of one cup of very bad coffee, a piece of hoe cake or fried dough, made of grease and white flour; and three small pieces of fried pork sides (sometimes called middlings) and some Georgia sorghum. This was the best meal of the day and was eaten ravenously by all but the new convicts. A spoon, tin cup, and tin plate, were the only implements. The spoon was always carried—attached to the belt by a piece of leather, or was stuck in one of the leg belts.

After breakfast we assembled in the yard, which was enclosed with two separate fences of barbed wire. The Warden of Fulton County Chain Gang (that is where I now was) stood by the door, and as the convicts filed past him into the yard, he would holler "*Come by me. Come by me. Come by me.*"

We then assembled in the yard in groups of about twenty in each group; two guards to each group. We stood two by two, each with the iron ring on the upright chain in his hand and towards the side of the man next to him. A guard would then run a chain down through the center of the group, passing the chain through each iron ring held in the hand of each convict. This chain was known as the "squad chain" and when locked in place (through each iron ring of each convict) we were all chained together and we could only go about five feet from our nearest sufferer.

There were about one hundred white men at this camp and we assembled in five groups each morning.

After being chained together—or on the squad chain— each group climbed into one truck. Those who could get in first sat down either on the floor or sides, while the rest of the group stood up. The two guards sat on the front seat with the driver. Each guard carried a pistol and an automatic shotgun. As the truck passed out through the gate each group was counted and checked.

This whole process was carried out in the early morning darkness, lighted only by flare torches which gave the whole a touch of weirdness. Leaving the gate we continued our ride in darkness. Upon arriving at the scene of our labors, we unloaded and waited for dawn to furnish enough light for us to begin work.

My group worked in a quarry, drilling holes with sledge hammer and steel drill, in which dynamite would be later exploded, or breaking up large stone, or shoveling up sproul (small pieces of stone).

We were all chained together on the squad chain while we worked, making it impossible for anyone to run away, unless he cut one of the chains first.

The guards were illiterate and coarse and brutal—never being satisfied with our work and always threatening us with "getting our—knocked off" by the Warden when we got back to the camp at night. Any reply whatsoever except "Yes, sir" was sure to provoke an additional stream of abuse from the guards.

Even as I write this meager description of a Georgia chain gang, I realize words or language cannot give an exact presentation of the malicious, cold brutality which we encountered. One was never allowed to rest a moment but must always be hard at work, and even moving in the mass of chain was painful and tiring—yet if one did not keep up his work greater terrors and more brutal punishment was in reserve. If a convict wanted to stop for a second to wipe the sweat off his face, he would have to call out "Wiping it off" and wait until the guard replied, "Wipe it off" before he could do so.

About every hour or so a water boy (usually a trusty or some prisoner whose time was almost out) would come around with a pail of water and give each convict a drink.

We commenced work about 5 A.M. and were still at it until 11:30 A.M. when the guard called out "Lay 'em down" (meaning lay down the tools and eat).

Dinner came out in a galvanized iron bucket. Tin plates were in a wooden box and another box contained corn pone, cut in six-inch squares. Each convict grabbed a tin plate and a square of corn pone, and one of the convicts, using his plate as a dipper, dished out the contents of the iron bucket as each convict presented his tin plate.

The contents of the iron bucket was boiled, dried cowpeas (not eaten anywhere else but in Georgia) and called "red beans." They were unpalatable, full of sand and worms.

This was our dinner—red beans and corn pone. The corn pone was heavy, bitter, and also very unpalatable. And needless to say, the whole arrangement was unsanitary, and filthy.

Dinner eaten, we lay down at full length—right where we happened to be, and rested and smoked if we had anything to smoke.

At one o'clock we were roused by the guards calling out "Let's go back." And back to work we'd go.

The afternoon was a repetition of the morning—the convicts laboring as hard as they could, the chains clanking, and the guards cursing and finding fault with each convict.

Finally, just as the sun was sinking in the West, about 6 P.M., and the prisoners were about sunk also, the guard called out again "Lay 'em down." The day's work was over.

A truck appeared and we loaded up again and started back to camp. Once there, we were unlocked from the chain and lined up in single file in front of the door to the wooden building. Each convict was searched and his chains and shackles examined before entering; and as he went in he "counted off"—the first one in line would count "one," the next, "two," etc.

All of us were dirty, sweaty, exhausted. There were three tin basins for one hundred men to wash in—there were no towels—any old piece of cloth or an old bag was pressed into service by the few who did get time to wash. As soon as all groups were safely in the building (usually about five minutes elapsed from the time the first group came in until the last group arrived, thereby only giving the first group in the building barely enough time to wash) supper was served. This was announced by a guard yelling "Come and get it" or "Get your feed," and we all filed into the mess hall.

The mess hall was simply a lot of long plain wooden tables similar to those seen at picnic grounds, and wooden benches. Because of our chains an end seat on the bench was at a premium. Those who sat in the middle of the bench, had to first sit with their back to the table and then swing around—not being able to step over the bench because of the chains.

Supper consisted of another square of corn pone, another three slices of fried pig fat and another dose of sorghum.

The menu as stated here *never varied*. It is identical for 362 days of the year, the only change being on July 4, Thanksgiving and Christmas, and on Sundays when there were only two meals, the dinner of red beans being eliminated.

The kitchen and mess hall of every chain gang is a disgrace. The word filthy does not begin to cover it, sanitation being unknown.

After supper we filed back into the sleeping section and each man lay down on his bunk. This is simply an iron cot, a dirty mattress, a still dirtier pillow, and a filthy blanket.

Before being put on the building chain, the Warden comes in with the head guard of each group. Each guard picks out one or more men from his group who he claims did not work hard enough. The first night I was there six convicts were selected. These were brought into the mess hall. Silence reigned supreme in the sleeping quarters. There was a tenseness in the air—everyone felt it. As the mess hall was separated from the sleeping quarters only by steel bars, we could all hear and partly see what took place.

We heard a voice speaking to one of the six:

"So, you son of a bitch, you won't work, eh? Get your pants down."

The convict started to speak—to say something in his defense—but it was drowned out. Strong hands grabbed hold of him, pulled down his pants, baring his buttocks, and then laid him face downward on one of the benches. He was held down so that he could not move. A leather strap six feet long, three inches wide, one-quarter inch thick was brought forth. The wielder of this instrument of torture stood off from the convict, judging his distance with a practised eye. He growled at the convict:

"So you won't work, eh? Well, damn you, I'll learn you to work on this chain gang!"

And with a terrific crash, the heavy strap came down on bare flesh with all the strength of the wielder behind it. The convict let out a yell—pleaded for mercy—promised to work—promised anything, but the strap rose again and descended with a sickening crash, the force of which temporarily shut off the pleadings of the convict. And so it went—one, two, three, four, five, six, seven, eight, nine, ten. Ten licks and the convict, half fainting or perhaps unconscious, was stood up on his feet—blood running down his legs, and one of the guards carried or led him back into the sleeping quarters.

The next five got the same dose.

The men who had been whipped had been given no medicine for their bleeding wounds. The guard ran the building chain through our iron rings, the lights went out, and silence again, except now and then a convict getting up to use the toilets—and the clanking and banging of chains in the darkness and his call and the guard's reply. And lastly, the agonized groans of the six who had been beaten.

Thus went my first day in the chain gang. And fear and despair clutched my weary heart. Was this a nightmare? Was it the hell I once read of in "Revelations," or was I going insane?

CHAPTER IV

A Decision to Run Out

I WAS exhausted mentally, physically, and spiritually, and soon fell asleep. I thought I had been asleep about five minutes when I was awakened at 3:30 by the building chain being pulled through my ring.

Each day was an exact duplicate of the one preceding it. Only some nights more of us or fewer "got the leather," as it was called.

The dirty filthy "stripes" would stick to the wounds on the buttocks and cause inflammation and torture.

And that is what a chain gang is for, torture! Torture every day. Any idea of reformation, any idea of trying to innoculate ideas of decency, manners, or good and right thinking in the convict, is prohibited. All the convicts get is abuse, curses, punishment, and filth. In a few weeks all are reduced to the same level, just animals, and treated worse than animals.

I did not wash my hands and face, or comb my hair or change my clothes until Saturday, when we got a bath. A piece of borax soap about as large as a package of chewing gum was given to each convict to bathe with, and a clean suit of "stripes."

I traded a square plug of chewing tobacco for a shave. Tobacco is rationed twice a week—a plug of chewing on Wednesdays and smoking tobacco on Saturdays.

Personal hygiene or cleanliness was impossible. Cleaning your teeth was out of the question entirely, except on Saturdays or Sundays.

Sunday we were all locked in the building; but we were allowed to rest until about 8 o'clock. This rest on Sunday morning was the only comfort one could find on the chain gang. Less than twenty per cent of the prisoners could read, so reading matter was scarce, and time to read scarcer, it being limited to Saturday evenings and Sundays.

So much for the Fulton County chain gang as it was then in 1922. What it's like now, I don't know. I take my oath that I have described it exactly—but mere words can never convey the true conditions as they were, the utter hopelessness and torture the convict suffers.

15

I have been in three different chain gangs (140 counties of the 161 counties in Georgia have them). State convicts are leased to these counties for their board and keep, with the County Warden in absolute command. Conditions are almost identical on all, as I found out later.

So many prisoners died from the beatings they received that Governor Walker of Georgia was obliged to abolish the leather in 1923 to still the national agitation against this medieval brutality.

The chain gang is simply a vicious, medieval custom, inherited from the blackbirders and slave traders of the seventeenth and eighteenth centuries, and is so archaic and barbarous as to be a national disgrace.

There was a saying on the chain gang, and it ran as follows:

"Work out"—meaning make your time.

"Pay out"—meaning purchase a pardon or parole.

"Die out"—meaning to die—or

"Run out"—meaning to escape.

I pondered on these four means of release. I had been a soldier and suffered torture and taken chances with my life for my country. Such studied torture as this, however, was too much for me. Death would have been a welcome relief. And so I pondered more and more each day. "Work out" was out of the question. Six years of this and I would return to society a worthless, defeated creature, unhuman and inhumane. "Pay out." By listening to the conversation of the native Georgians and old-timers, I found that $2,000 was the average price with which to "pay out" or buy freedom. And even then the convict must first serve a year. My parents had no $2,000 and I'd be free or dead in less than a year. That I knew only too well.

Not that I wanted to cheat justice. I leave that to the reader. If I had been sentenced to one year—which under the conditions of the chain gang and the extenuating circumstances of my crime, would have been plenty—I would have tried to make it. But six years—that was plain vengeance and also complete destruction.

"Well," thought I—"Die out."

I'll "Die out" trying to "run out." That was the definite conclusion I finally came to after two weeks at Fulton County.

I had heard from other convicts that in the smaller counties they had fewer prisoners and perhaps more opportunities of escape.

Promptly the following Sunday I wrote a letter to the Prison Commissioners. This Commission is similar to the parole board of other states. In Georgia the Prison Commissioners function as a parole board and also as a supervisory force over the one hundred forty-odd County Wardens of the chain gangs. The Commission consists of three members. In my letter to them I asked for a transfer to some other county gang.

Two weeks later I was transferred with eleven other convicts to Campbell County chain gang. Prior to our arrival at this camp, the County Warden, Sam Parkins, would only accept "niggers" and there had been no white convicts there for several years.

Conditions here were almost the same as at Fulton County, with these exceptions: Our sleeping quarters were worse. Twelve men slept in a "pie wagon" (a steel-barred wagon on wheels, four tiers of three bunks each) and we barely had room to turn around. The mess hall was simply a shed built inside a barbed wire stockade, and there was no wash-room at all. We washed in the open from a bucket.

The nightly whippings took place in the yard—the convict being laid on a semi-circular piece of corrugated iron.

The "pie wagon" and bedding were lousy, full of vermin, and were old and decayed and had a foul odor.

We did not work on a squad chain as at Fulton County, as here we worked on the roads and were spread out a little more. We also worked with the Negroes.

Here, then, was a chance to run, if you could run with twenty pounds of chain or if you could remove the chain.

Blood-hounds were taken to the road each day and the guards were increased, two guards to each twelve convicts. For six weeks I racked my brain for a method of removing those chains. Two others of the twelve convicts in my group were also willing to take desperate measures to escape. One tried cutting the steel rivets in his shackles with an improvised saw made from a safety razor blade.

But as our chains and shackles were thoroughly examined once a day, he was discovered and received several terrific beatings. Besides, at night, we were so fatigued and exhausted that it was impossible to use any skill or strength for such delicate tasks.

At night, as we filed in through the entrance to the mess hall, blacks on one side, whites on the other, came a voice:

"Come by me—I want to smell you. Come by me—I want to smell you."

Meaning that the speaker wanted to smell the perspiration on each convict so as to be sure the convicts had "put out" a day of strenuous and fatiguing toil. If he didn't smell you, you got the leather.

From a thorough study of conditions I had also arrived at this conclusion: Any escape would have to be made on a Monday morning, for that would be the only time in the week that one would have the strength to hope for success. The rest on Sunday would refresh and quicken the brain—but by Tuesday morning this would vanish, and for the balance of the week the convict would go through his daily labors in almost a semi-conscious state—so great was the exhaustion and fatigue from the heat and long hours of toil.

That was the first fact I planted in my brain—*Monday morning when I was fresh*—some Monday morning—when? But Monday morning it must be! No other time would I try.

The next problem was the chains. How to get these off—when and where I wanted them off. Finally this idea struck me. The shackles around my ankles were circular in shape. I knew if they could be bent into an elliptical shape, that perhaps I could slip them over my heel, after removing my shoes. But how to bend them? That was a difficulty, for they were made of steel as thick as a man's finger.

Day in and day out—every conscious moment I studied, planned and discarded, planned anew, discarded again— plans—plans—but all seemed idle dreams. And thousands of convicts the whole world over are all dreaming the same dream: a successful escape from the tortures and obsolete treatment modern society deals out to its weaker element.

CHAPTER V

Breaking the Shackles

O
NE DAY I noticed a certain Negro in my group swing a twelve-pound sledge hammer. He had been in the gang so long and had used a sledge so much that he had become an expert. Claimed he could hit a pin on the head with his eyes closed.

Suddenly, like a flash, an idea came to me. I might try to get that Negro to hit my shackles and bend them into an elliptical shape. If I could put my leg against something to take up the shock and hold the shackle against it. I determined to think this over.

Of course, if I were discovered, many brutal beatings were in store for me.

A week later we were tearing up an old railroad, ties, rails and all. And there was my answer—I could place my foot against the end of a railroad tie that was still embedded in the road ballast. This would give the support needed. The Negro could hit the shackle and perhaps it would bend. If he missed the shackle, it would mean perhaps the loss of a foot. Not pleasant thoughts, but life-or-death problems call for both daring and courage.

I maneuvered things so that I worked near this Negro at all times, waiting for a chance to speak to him.

One day in June, when the heat was terrific and the guards were half asleep from the humidity, I spoke to him.

"Sam," I said. "Would you do me a favor?"

"Boss, if I can, I sho' will," he replies.

"Sam, I got six years; that's a long time, and I'm going to try to 'hang it on the limb,' and I need a little help. Will you help me?" I asked.

"Boss, it sho' is pretty rough, and I ain't much for hunting trouble, but if I's can help you, I sho' will," he answered.

"Well, Sam, here's the idea—if I put my leg against this tie—do you think you could hit my shackle hard enough to bend it and still not break my ankle?" I asked.

"Boss, if you can keep the shackle from turning, I can hit it right

19

plump," he answered.

I looked up at the two guards; all was quiet and serene. I put my right foot against the tie—by spreading my legs the connecting chain became taut—one side of the shackle against the tie. I looked at Sam. He grinned. I looked at the guards. All was as it should be. I took a deep breath, closed my eyes, and said to Sam, "Shoot, Sam." Sam shot. Bang went the sledge; I felt a sharp quick pain in my shins. One side of the shackle was embedded in the end of the tie. I looked at the shackle, but couldn't see much difference in the shape. Another look at the guards. All was well. "Again, Sam," I whispered. Another bull's-eye by Sam. "Again, Sam," I said. And again the sledge fell right on the shackle. Then the left foot. Three solid whacks of the sledge on the left shackle.

"Thanks, Sam," I said. "If they won't come off now we'll try again."

Night could not come quick enough. Would the shackles come off? Would the guard discover the change from circular to elliptical, when examining the chains when we returned for the night?

The day was over at last, supper finished and we were lined up single file in front of the "pie wagon," to be searched and our chains inspected. My heart was beating hard and fast. My turn came, I was searched, the chains were examined, I counted off and passed on. What a relief!

Ten minutes later, lying on my bunk, I tried to pass the shackle over my heel. What a thrill! *It would come off!* A little tight, but it would come off. Wet it with a little saliva and it would come off. This was Wednesday night. Monday was the day! Four days to lay my plans—four days till Monday. Monday was my day!

I had four dollars and twenty cents. The rules of the chain gang permitted the prisoners to receive money. All mail was opened by the Warden, he was the censor and the banker. If the family or friends of the convicts sent them any money the Warden would allow them as much as $2.00 per week of the funds sent. My family was sending me $2.00 each week. This $4.20 was saved by me from that allowance. Perhaps by Saturday or Sunday I would have a letter with $2.00 more. That would be $6.20. Sunday morning the Warden handed me a letter and the $2.00 was there. So much the better.

Now for the new difficulties. There were the bloodhounds; three of them, with us all of the time. In discussing means of escape, the native hillbillies fear the dogs. They would say, "You got to get off the ground, or the dogs will get you. You got to get off the ground or you can't make it because the dogs will be upon you in ten minutes. They are trained to howl and bite and betray you. You got to get off the ground." I listened to this but kept my own counsel.

Then there were the clothes to secure. Also, I was a Northerner and my speech would betray me. I didn't know the country. Georgia is a large state, sparsely populated, and a stranger with a Northern accent stands out and can be easily recognized. The guards also carry repeating shotguns and shoot at you too, that much was certain.

The whole thing presented many obstacles that seemed impossible to overcome. Frankly I estimated my chances at one to one hundred. But here again my army training and war experiences came to my rescue. A hundred times I had missed death by a hair over in France—I had seen my buddies die—death ended their troubles. Now they were sleeping peacefully. I'd shake dice with Fate and try to take advantage of every opportunity. Monday I was going—it was to be death, freedom, or capture. No matter how the die was cast, I couldn't have been much worse off than I was then.

Monday morning, June 21, 1922—the longest and hottest day of the year—we left the camp at 4 A.M. Twelve convicts, two guards and three blood-hounds.

Our job that day was tearing up a small wooden bridge over a creek about twelve feet wide. By 10:30 it was all up; only one stringer was still in place. Three convicts, one guard, and myself were on one side of the stream. The other guard, nine convicts and the dogs were on the other. The bridge served as a link in the county road which crossed the creek here. On either side of the road were bushes and shrubbery about four feet high. Back of the road were the hinterlands of Georgia. Pine-covered hills, corn and cotton fields on the flats, bayous and swamps in the lowlands.

When it was necessary for a convict to obey the call of nature while working on the road he sang out to the guard, "Getting out here," and then waited for the guard to answer. The guard would look over both sides of the road, select a particular spot and answer, "All right, get out here," and point to the spot. Not over two to three minutes were allowed, and the guards were then on the alert and watched the convict closely.

My heart was in my mouth, I was nervous and taut, my face was drawn—my voice rang out, "Getting out here." I was startled at the sound of it. My hour had struck. A chilly fear crept up my spine.

"All right, 'Shorty,' get out here, and don't be long," came back the guard's reply.

Laying down my pick, I glanced at the other guard, fifty feet away. Everything seemed regular and usual.

I went into the bushes, sat down, took off my shoes, slipped off the chains, put on my shoes, then on my hands and knees, Indian fashion, I started to crawl away. I kept crawling, hidden by the underbrush.

The two minutes were up. The guards called out, "Come on, Shorty, get back to work."

I was supposed to answer, "Yes, sir." If I didn't answer the guard would call for the dogs. If I did answer the guard could tell from the direction of my voice that I had moved from the place he designated. So when he called, "Come on, Shorty," I jumped to my feet and like a flash I broke into a run. The guard was startled, surprised, and I gained a few precious seconds. I ran at top speed, never looking back. Suddenly I heard the crack of the shotgun, *bang!*

Buckshot flew all around. I put on more speed. The cry went up, "Shorty's gone, bring on the dogs." Bang, bang! went the gun; but I was going like the wind and with the last shot I was under cover of the woods.

Never in my life did I run as I did that day. Ten minutes later the dogs were at my heels, howling, barking, and snapping. But instead of being afraid of them I talked to them, I called them and tried to make them think I was playing with them. I kept to the woods and fields using the sun as my guide to point north.

CHAPTER VI

Running the Gauntlet through Georgia

AFTER TWENTY minutes I broke into a steady gait, the dogs still at my heels. Through bushes, briars, hills, dales, fields, swamps, and small streams I ran. The heat was terrific; I was burning up, and when I came to a stream, I lay in it full length for a second, taking a long drink. Refreshed, I started again, only to be scorched by the heat once more.

How light my feet and legs felt! For the first time in twelve weeks I was not carrying a twenty-pound chain.

All morning I kept going, never stopping but to drink for a second or two when I struck water. I was tired, exhausted, ready to quit, but this was not a race, this was life or death! Somehow I called on tired muscles, heaving lungs, a pumping heart, and they answered my agonized plea, and responded when I thought they were through. What a race I ran that day.

It was about 5 P.M. and I was still going strong, through fields, woods, and swamps, and the dogs still with me, barking, howling, but apparently enjoying it immensely, for by this time they were my friends.

I came through a wood to a small clearing occupied by a Negro shanty. There were clothes hanging on a line. A Negro woman was bending over a wash-tub beside the shanty. I needed clothes. I ran up to the line, grabbed a pair of overalls and a man's shirt, and kept right on going, still heading North. Entering another small patch of woods I changed clothes. The overalls were much too large, and so was the shirt.

At about 6 o'clock, I struck a railroad trestle over a small river. I was so hot and so exhausted, having been on the run since morning, that this river looked like Paradise.

I couldn't resist the temptation of a cool plunge. Crossing the trestle to the center I jumped in, feet first, and started swimming slowly downstream. The dogs were dismayed by this turn of affairs, but followed along the bank. I stayed in the water about half an hour, still swimming downstream. By this time the dogs were quiet. They were somewhere back along the bank.

Crawling out of the river on the opposite side from which I had left the dogs, I started walking North again. Walking was quite a relief from running, and it gave me time to think. I was refreshed physically now from my great exertion, but it was still unbearably hot. So hot, in fact, that in ten minutes my clothes were practically dry.

Unexpectedly at about 7 o'clock I came to a paved highway. Paved highways are rare in Georgia, so I knew this must be leading me to some large city. Considerable automobile traffic was flowing both ways. Seeing this I made an instant decision. I'd go out on this highway, flag some auto, and get a ride going in any direction. The direction wouldn't make any difference, I had to keep moving and get as far away from the camp as possible. To think was to act. I was on the road. A young man in a Ford coupé stopped to pick me up. On the door of the car, in small letters were the words, "Standard Oil Company."

I got in. In order to sit down I had to pick up a large basket of peaches which was on the seat beside him, and hold the basket in my lap. The peaches looked so inviting, and I must have looked at them so longingly, that he said to me, "Eat a couple of them if you want."

"Thanks," I answered.

As I started to eat a peach, I wondered where he was going, and, afraid he'd ask me where I was going, I quickly framed the following question: "How far are you going?"

"Atlanta," he answered.

"Fine," I came back. "If you have no objections I'll thank you if I can go all the way with you."

"Sure," he answered. "But it isn't far, only about nine miles."

Nine miles! I must have covered about twenty-seven miles in my cross-country run.

As I ate the peach, speculating on what I'd do in Atlanta, two autos full of police, shotguns sticking out of the sides, whizzed by, going in the opposite direction. I recognized Chief Beavers himself in the first car with all his gold braid.

"I wonder who they're after," my friend said.

"Moonshiners," I answered, with my heart in my mouth.

Before I knew it we were in Atlanta. It was almost 8 o'clock. We passed a General Clothing store. The sign read, "I. Cohen & Son." The store was still open. I got out at the next corner, and went into the store.

I bought a suit of overalls, pants, and a jumper that fit, and a fifty-cent cotton shirt, and changed clothes in the store. This set me back $2.50. I still had $3.70 left. Not much to get away on.

I went into a barber shop to get a shave. While I was being shaved a policeman came in. He was a regular customer and knew the barbers. After hanging up his coat and hat he said, "A New York gunman escaped from the Campbell County gang this morning. There are several posses out after him and I guess they'll get him!"

I couldn't see the speaker as I lay flat on my back, my face full of soap lather. A nervous tremor ran through my body, beads of perspiration started to roll down me, but I just sat tight.

The barber asked, "What does he look like?"

And the cop answered, "About thirty years old and a short stocky man, as near as I can find out. We have orders out to watch all railroads, bus stations, and exits from the city. They think he is heading toward Atlanta."

And there I sat in the chair, staring at the ceiling. Fear clutched every nerve and muscle. If I attracted suspicion I was done for. The barber finished and I got out of the chair. My legs were trembling and I was a nervous wreck. Without speaking I handed the barber a half dollar. He gave me thirty-five cents change. I took it and tried to walk as casually as possible to my jumper and black "gin house Stetson" cotton hat, hanging on the clothes rack. That hat was a prison hat, almost new, but it looked the same as any black felt hat. Would the copper notice this? If he had asked me any question I think I would have collapsed. How I got out of that barber shop without creating any suspicion I don't know. I was in a daze when I reached the street. I kept turning corners zig-zag fashion, and did not even breathe freely until I got about five blocks away.

After eating a cheap meal I entered a cheap hotel. The sign read, *Rooms 75¢ and Up.* I had to get off the streets and rest, and think of my next move. The hotel building was three stories high. The entire ground floor was occupied by a store. The hotel began on the second floor. I went up and in.

The clerk looked me over in startled surprise. "So you 'hung it on the limb,' eh?" he exclaimed. I looked at him, startled and dumbfounded. It so happened that he had been finishing a twelve-month sentence for narcotics at Sandy Springs chain gang when I first went there, and he recognized me instantly.

Knowing what the chain gang was like, and having nothing but hatred for the law, he was glad to see I had beaten a six-year rap. He rushed me into his own room and wanted to know how I had done it. After questions and answers on both sides, I learned I had unconsciously walked into "a polite joint," to use his phrase. It was running under cover, but had both political and police protection.

After the formalities were over he offered me whiskey or dope, but I wanted none of it. He was anxious to please me and thought I was quite a fellow to have beaten the chain gang, especially when I was wearing a twenty-pound chain. He offered me all the money he had, six dollars, which I accepted.

He left the room for a couple of minutes and came back with two "broads."

"Girls," he said, "here's a real guy. He just hung six years on the limb, and ain't seen a girl for the last three months. Anything you do for him is on the house."

This floored me completely. I didn't want any women, and I wanted to conserve my strength. I wanted to get out of Dixie. I also began to realize that my affable friend was a "junker." I began to get real worried. This guy would be bringing everybody into the joint to see me next. So I spoke up.

"Say, buddie, please don't bring any more people to see me. I want to get out of Atlanta, and out of Dixie, and I am not looking for a good time. People talk, unconsciously sometimes, and the first thing you know I'll get grabbed."

"All right," he said. "I'll leave you here with the girls and I won't bother you any more; if you want anybody just ring," pointing to a push button on the wall.

But I didn't want the girls either, so I said:

"Girls, you got me sized up wrong. I am no goodie-goodie, but I am no professional criminal either, and I don't intend to go on breaking the law, or following any racket. All I want is to get out of Atlanta and Dixie, get some job and be on the square."

With this one of the girls went out, wishing me luck; but the other came over and sat down on the bed beside me.

"Gee," she said, "you're what I call a real guy. I wish I could hook up with some man with guts like you, get out of this damn racket, and go straight once more. If I help you to get out of Atlanta will you take me with you?"

I felt sorry for her; such a pity, I thought, for she was fairly good looking, and about twenty-five years old. But—"He travels fastest who travels alone," so I politely explained to her that such a course was impossible. However, I compromised by telling her that if she would help me and I got through o. k., I would send for her and help her go straight.

She eagerly accepted the proposition and asked me how she could help. She was all excited and thrilled. I must have touched something in her when I declared myself for "the straight and narrow" instead of "the free and easy" path.

She said, "I am glad to help anyone who has will and strength enough to determine to be on the level. I have tried so hard myself to break away, but somehow I always slip back. If I had someone to help me and stand by me for a while, I think I could make it. Anyway, I am going to try and help you to get through."

With this she went into the "first national," and handed me nine bucks—her entire roll.

"Take it, kid," she said, "and don't worry about me, I'll get more before the night's over. You'll need it far worse than me." Next she opened her handbag, wrote her name and address on the back of some Atlanta business man's card and handed it to me, saying: "When you get set, send for me."

I sent her out for time tables, as I wanted to find out where and when I could catch a train at some nearby town going north. In a little while she came back with a time table of every railroad leaving Atlanta.

We discussed every line of travel out of Atlanta, and I tried to figure out something to fit the time tables.

At last I decided on the following plan: The Nashville, Chattanooga and St. Louis Railroad had a train passing through Marietta about 8:45 A.M., going to Chattanooga, Tennessee. From the girl I learned that there was a trolley leaving Atlanta at 6 A.M. that arrives at Marietta at 8:30 A.M. It was the best I could figure out and I decided to go through with it, come what may.

I had a hard time getting rid of the girl as she was anxious to please me. But I wanted sleep and rest and strength and a clear head for tomorrow's troubles. She finally left, however, saying she'd come back and wake me at 5:30 in the morning.

Alone at last, I bolted the door, took off my shoes, and lay down on the bed. Sleep was impossible—my mind was full of the problems ahead—I couldn't relax at all, just tossed and rolled. Finally, from sheer exhaustion I dozed off a little.

Sure enough at 5:30 the next morning my benefactress of the night before rapped on the door. When I let her in she had hot coffee in a little tin bucket, and a bag of hot biscuits. We sat down and ate together, then we left the place and she showed me where to get the trolley, bade me goodbye and got me to promise to send for her when I got settled. The trolley appeared at last. I thanked her and promised to send for her, said goodbye again and got on. Alas! I could not keep my promise, for I lost the card with her address before I ever got settled.

The trolley arrived at Marietta at 8:15 instead of 8:30. I had half an hour to wait for the train. Too long to stay in such a small town. Also I remembered that this was the place where Leo M. Frank had been lynched. He was a New York Jew. The thought sent another quiver of fear through my nervous system. But in a flash I got hold of myself. I had to get through. A cool head and calm nerves, brain power, quick thinking and quicker action should give me an even break.

These thoughts went through my brain as I got off the trolley. In the one swift survey I took in the town square. I saw a Woolworth 5 & 10. A Negro was sweeping the pavement in front of the store. That told me the store was open. In the same glance I saw the only railroad station, the Nashville, Chattanooga and St. Louis Railroad.

In that one glance my plans were laid and made. Boldly I walked to the station and purchased a ticket for Chattanooga. At the station I saw the train was chalked up five minutes late. From the station I went direct to the 5 & 10 cent store. I had to kill almost thirty-five minutes in this store. I kept wandering around the counters, one eye on the entrance, and on all persons who entered. At last, in sheer desperation I spent the last few minutes there buying a ten cent ring. I left the store at 8:45, walking slowly but deliberately toward the station. Fifty feet from the station was a small Coca Cola and hot dog stand. Still no train. The one place I couldn't wait for the train was at the station. Someone might ask questions. So I stopped at this stand and got a "dope" (as they call Coca Cola in Georgia).

While I was drinking, a horse and buggy pulled up at the station. The lone driver was a man in uniform with a large black soft hat. I asked the man in the stand who it was.

"The Chief of Police," he answered.

"Does he always come down to see the train in," I asked.

"No," he replied. "This is something unusual for him to do. He must be expecting someone, or looking for someone."

Another shock hit my nerves. Trapped! This idea flashed through my brain—trapped! Before I could even think of some plan of action, I saw three more men come over and talk to the Chief. The man behind the counter broke my reverie with:

"Hot dog! Something's up. Half the police force is down to meet the train."

I must think! I must act! I heard the train's approaching whistle. I couldn't stay in Marietta and I couldn't go down to the station. Oh! where was that quick thinking brain power now? Now when I needed it most, my brain failed to even direct a muscle. I was rooted to the spot.

Again the train's warning whistle for the grade crossing. In a few seconds it would be here! The sound of that approaching train finally cleared my brain. I couldn't bring myself to attempt to get out of Georgia by following highways. Georgia is a very large state. Furthermore, my speech was sure to betray me. I spoke the English language "a la New York." It jars the ears of Georgians. They can spot it in an instant! It would take a week to get out of Georgia by highway, and I'd be sure to get caught. No! the train was my only hope. And somewhere my brain dug up from memory in that trying moment, a quotation from Goethe, "Courage has magic, power, and genius in it." The passage seemed to be the answer to my problem.

Perhaps it might be true—I'd try it out!

Gathering all my strength for this supreme task, I started to walk boldly towards the station and the train which was now pulling in.

CHAPTER VII

To Chicago and—Freedom!

I HAD NOT gone twenty-five feet when I heard loud cries coming from the station.

"There he is! There he is! Get him!"

My heart jumped right into my throat! There was awful excitement and bustle at the station. Men were running. They were chasing someone. But that someone was not me! It seems that a hobo was on that train. As it pulled in, someone saw him. He saw them first. He got off and ran, and all the police, and hangers-on started after him. All this happened in an instant. I had a clear road to the train. I took it, walked down and got on the train. Even when I got on the train, the crew, interested in what was taking place, didn't notice me. I boarded the last car of the train and sat down. From the station I heard cries, "They got him. They got him all right." More excitement, everyone at the station, crowded around the captive, people in the train crowded to the station side to stick their heads out of the windows.

The proud captor brought the victim to the Chief. Everybody was asking his neighbor what was up. The Chief was speaking to the victim. Everyone was quiet now, waiting with an air of expectancy for the Chief to finish questioning him.

Suddenly the Chief cried out, "This isn't the man we want. This is the wrong man." More excitement. Dissatisfaction and defeat were written on everyone's face. The wrong man! And then the news rushed through the small crowd as those close to the Chief heard the conversation and passed it on. The talk ran as follows: A convict had escaped yesterday. He was a vicious gunman from New York. The police in Atlanta had gotten a tip that he would be on this train. When the hobo turned out to be a native Georgian, and, besides, didn't fit the description, everybody was disappointed.

However, the train was late. Now it was still later, and the N. C. & St. Louis Railroad was a single-track road. The conductor was all business again. He called out, "all aboard," gave the signal, and we started.

31

As the wheels started to turn, back in the last car sat a still-faced little man in overalls. He sat so still you'd think he was a statue. Finally, as the train picked up momentum and left the station, if you were still looking at him, you'd think the statue had turned to powder and collapsed. In fact, not until the train was going thirty miles an hour did I even dare to breathe. Talk about breaks! If anyone ever got a break, it was I who got one in Marietta.

It was a beautiful day. The sun was shining brightly. I was on my way to freedom! I was free! Click, clack, click, clack! Free at last!

With a bang, I was brought back to my senses.

"Ticket, please." It was the conductor. I handed him my ticket. He looked at it. He looked at me. His look told me volumes.

"Where did you get on?" he asked me.

"Marietta," I answered. But he knew where I had gotten on as well as I myself did—only *he hadn't seen me get on.* He punched the ticket, gave me a colored slip and looked worried. So was I. Plenty worried!

The conductor engaged the brakeman in a conversation and they both stole glances in my direction.

And there I sat, dazed again by this sudden turn of affairs. Good God! Would I ever get away? Could a nervous system stand any more shocks and still survive and function. Would this fearful suspense never let up. By sheer force of a tired and battered will I brought myself to consider the situation.

I *was* riding on this train. The conductor and the crew were suspicious of me. They had heard the excitement at Marietta. So had I. I was under suspicion. What was I to do? I figured and thought and worried. I couldn't plan anything. We were still in Georgia. To leave the train would change suspicion to a certainty. Well, I had gotten this far by courage. I'd sit tight and let *them* make the first move. But I couldn't stop thinking and thinking. If I got off I would surely be caught. If I stayed on I'd get caught in Chattanooga before I left the station. I tried to give my mind a rest for a little while so I could try and think clearly after the mental rest. But my mind wouldn't rest. In sheer desperation I took a time-table from the little rack by the window and started to look through it. I saw the table of the train I was on. Unconsciously I began to study that table. I noticed a small town (whose name I have forgotten) listed as a stop a few miles over the Tennessee border, and it was also the last stop before Chattanooga. That was my station. When the train got there I was going to get off. But the conductor and the crew must not be aware of my intention.

Quickly I formed a plan which was as follows: I would take a seat near the door. When the train pulled in I would stay in my seat. Just as the train started to leave I would jump up and get out. That was the best plan I could conjure. That was what I would do. What a strain those four hours in that train were.

But the plan was successful and there I was, walking on the highway toward Chattanooga. Free! Free! Free! At last! How wonderful just to walk along the highway again in June. Yes, it was hot! But one does not feel the heat so much when one has toiled at back-breaking labor, wearing twenty pounds of chain. No one to curse you. No fear of the cruel and brutal lash after a day of toil. No! No! Only the birds singing sweetly in the bushes, and the leaves swaying lightly in the breeze. Birds and leaves sang one song to me that June afternoon. *Free! Free! Free!*

I have tasted almost every mental and physical thrill that man can feel, good and bad. But the thrill that I got that afternoon while hiking into Chattanooga will live in my memory forever. Free! I was sure of it. My mind felt it, intuition sensed it, the birds sang it. I *knew* it.

Chattanooga, Nashville, Louisville, Cincinnati, Indianapolis, Chicago! All the way by highway, with the exception of my trip from Louisville to Cincinnati by an Ohio River sidewheeler.

Nearing Chicago, I made a vow. No one knew me there. There's where I would settle down. Go to work! Any job, any price! Keep out of trouble! Honest labor—that was my only solution now.

CHAPTER VIII

An Unfortunate Marriage

STILL IN till in my fifty-cent cotton shirt, my overalls, "gin house" Stetson and all, with sixty cents in my pocket, I was in Chicago. At last! I had hitch-hiked a ride in a friendly auto and here I was.

I got out at Roosevelt Road and Crawford Avenue. I spent the day looking for a job in this vicinity, without success. Evening came and I had to have a place to sleep. I walked into the main part of the city, east along Roosevelt Road. At Kedzie Avenue soap-box spell-binders were holding a meeting. Each speaker when he finished passed the hat around. My entire wealth was twenty cents, a hat, shoes, shirt, and overalls. Night was approaching and I needed money. I listened to the spiel of one would-be orator. He passed the brown derby and collected. I was as good as he, I believed. One hour later, I was on the stand. I spoke for an hour. A great crowd gathered. After I had spoken for a while I passed the "gin house" Stetson and it came back with $3.85. I knew right then and there that I was going to like Chicago. More than that, I made up my mind to study the city, see it, know it, master it, and become a part of it.

The next day I worked in the Stock Yards at forty cents an hour—$3.20 a day—pay every night.

How peculiar is the human being. Two years before $3.20 a day was wage slavery—drudgery—a mere existence. Today, after the chain-gang experience, $3.20 a day was all that any man could want. It meant a clean bed, clean clothes, soap and towels, clean teeth, recreation, movies, books, libraries, lectures, walks through beautiful parks, museums, and the exhilaration of a great, growing, bustling city roaring all around, interesting and congenial people, things to see and do. In short, Life! I learned that $3.20 a day buys every comfort and necessity and many luxuries.

A year went by. I had changed jobs numerous times. North side, West side, South side; I had seen the city. I had learned to love it! its freedom from age-old tradition, its startling newness, its bustle, its growth, its perpetually varied forms of amusement, education, and recreation. A

Mecca for all! A million and a quarter visitors a week, its three million population extending its arms to all comers.

By some strange unknown power, I was filled with a desire to live in the Jackson Park area. I was now going to settle down, save money, and go into business.

And now, here comes destiny again! What part did Fate have in causing me to turn into Ingleside Avenue, looking for a room? And why did I stop at 6444 Ingleside Avenue where a small sign read, "ROOMS TO LET"?

I rang the bell. An old lady answered it. She couldn't speak English very well. She called someone; another woman came. I looked at a room, took it, and moved in. And this other woman, once my friend, was later to be fired with an insane hatred and a desire to cut me to ribbons, to tear down and destroy with tigerish ferocity, not only me, but all that I was to build up in the ensuing years. She it was who, in an instant, was to sweep away my reputation, business, wealth, love, romance, and happiness.

But that is life, I guess. To know happiness, sorrow must also be felt. To enjoy wealth, one must first feel the pangs of poverty. Love is not appreciated until the lover is gone.

This woman who showed me my room that day brought tragedy into my life, tragedy that neither time nor courage will ever erase. Is she happy now? I doubt it.

One week after moving in, I was on very familiar terms with Mrs. Emilia Del Pino Pacheo. She was a short, stout, dark-haired divorcee, of about forty years of age.

She was married, so I learned, at the early age of eighteen, to a cigar maker, a Joe Pacheo. This proved an unhappy marriage, and she was divorced a few years later. She, her sisters, and an aged mother had just bought the house. A few hundred dollars down, the balance in mortgages and monthly payments. She was employed as a dinner waitress from 11 A.M. to 2 P.M. at the Fred Harvey Sante Fe Lunch Room; $2.00 per day, and tips. This was the situation as I entered the picture.

In two months Emily had fallen hopelessly in love with me. She waited on my every want. Every artifice of woman, she used in her desperate struggle to capture my heart. She made life comfortable for me, tried to make me happy. She listened with eagerness to my schemes of business, which were either to start a hotel or a magazine. I became one of the family. What did I wish for Sunday dinner? Would I fix this or would I repair that? Would I look after this for her and her mother as they were not so familiar with the language or customs or laws?

Not being interested in any other woman, I accepted her with perhaps more than passing interest. After three months I saw how desperately in love this woman was. She admired me, looked up to me, believed in me. To her I was husband, lover and son. Husband, in exercising a certain influence and responsibility for the well being of the household and its members. Lover, in personifying all that she expected in the virile and dashing *bon vivant*. Son, when her maternal instinct came to the surface, when the eternal feminine desire to mother something, to possess and instruct and mold into her life, the thing that would always be denied her—motherhood. But I told her the blunt truth:

"Emily, I hate to tell you this, but I must. I like you, admire you, and appreciate your great interest in me, but I don't love you. Love is something that one must feel. I *know* I don't love you. I don't love you or any one right now—perhaps never will. I cannot will myself to love you, anymore than I can change the color of my eyes. Some day I may fall in love with another woman. Then I would be compelled to leave you. If you want to continue under these conditions, all right, but I shall never feel any different toward you. Perhaps I may never fall in love; in that case life with you will be as it is now, comfortable, pleasant, serene. But I am speaking plainly, bluntly, frankly. If romance blows the bugle I will have to say goodbye and fall in line."

It dampened her ardor—but only for a few days—when again she threw herself into the fight for my heart with all the charm, power and strength her Latin temperament could muster.

Because things were pleasant and comfortable I stayed on. Perhaps I would never fall in love again—so why worry and cause unnecessary trouble about something that might never happen?

I wanted to go into a business of my own to take advantage of the growth and wealth and opportunity that a big city presents. Either a hotel or a monthly magazine was attractive. Emily couldn't see the magazine— but a hotel—that she eagerly asserted she would be glad to help me with.

About this time I wrote to my father and brother, asking them to see if something couldn't be done to square things up in Georgia. This they tried to do but the result was discouraging. They wrote to me telling me of the failure of their efforts.

During all this time I had never received a letter from anyone addressed to me at 6444 Ingleside Avenue. Emily was always curious to learn something about me and my past. I always found a way of evading the issue or putting her off.

Early one evening she came up to my room carrying a letter, which she handed to me. I noticed at once by the post mark and handwriting that it was from my father. I looked at it, and the letter looked as though it had been opened. This made me nervous and apprehensive of danger. I asked Emily, "Did you notice that this letter looks as though it had been opened?"

"Yes," she said.

"Was it delivered that way?" I inquired.

"No," she said, "it was not. I opened it. That letter makes you my man for life."

I opened the letter, read it, and saw that anyone reading it would know my secret at once. I was undecided as to what to do. Would I leave Chicago at once? Would my secret come out in some unexplained manner wherever I settled down?

While I was pondering over this new difficulty, Emily came over to me, put her arms around me and kissed me lovingly. "Your secret is safe with me," she promised. "I love you and I am sorry for you. No matter what should happen between us, I promise faithfully never to betray you. Why," she said, "I love you so much that I would suffer terribly if any harm should ever come to you. Never, never, never, will I tell a single soul."

"But," I answered, "I don't love you the way you desire, and some day you may change your mind."

"Elliott," she answered, "I'm going to be so good and nice to you that some day you will love me. And even if you don't, I will always love you, and because I love you, you know I will never betray you."

And so, not wanting to leave Chicago and give up the friends and progress I had made there, I accepted her promise of silence and remained.

In 1924 we rented a large apartment at 930 East 65th Street, just around the corner from her home. She had $75 in cash—I had the same—and also the ideas and the plans. I would install sinks, gas ranges, and so alter this one apartment into several small, daintily furnished apartments.

This we did, purchasing used furniture at very low prices, repairing and re-varnishing each piece to fit into a definite scheme of decoration for each apartment. These two-room kitchenette apartments soon became the talk of the neighborhood. We made money. In six months we had rented the entire building at 930 and 932 East 65th Street. Emily looked after the linens, etc. I took care of the financial end.

After one year of this I decided to go into the publishing business with my share of the profits from the apartments. Running the apartments we were partners, dividing income and responsibility. However, the living expenses of both of us came out of my share. She lived with me as though she were my wife. This you will please understand was not objectionable to me, but was absolutely voluntary on her part.

In August, 1925, I started *The Greater Chicago Magazine*—alone—and with a very limited capital. Quickly my capital was consumed, also my income from the apartments. I still needed money. There were eighteen apartments—nine hers, and nine mine. Her share of the income was saved or put into paying off the mortgages at 6444 Ingleside Avenue. Besides, I was still paying both her own and my own living expenses.

Emily had taken a course in beauty culture, graduated, and I changed a front ground floor room at 930 East 65th Street into a small beauty parlor. This added slightly to her income, but her customers were never numerous, and her rates were considerably below the usual charges.

I had sunk a lot of money in the magazine—everyone said I was foolish—it couldn't be made to pay. I needed thousands to put over such a venture, and alas! I no longer even had tens.

I sold Emily *my* nine apartments. I borrowed from the Morris Plan, and still I needed more. Who will ever know the struggle, the sleepless nights, the days and months and years of seemingly hopeless effort I put into that business. But I would not give up—I must have money. I hung on when failure glared me straight in the face, when I was hemmed in by an overwhelming defeat. But still I hung on and carried on even when I could see nothing but black despair.

In the meantime my supervision over the eighteen apartments had ceased entirely. They became run down, dilapidated, people did not pay their rents, the income began to fall off, and Emily, not being equal to the task of running them alone, decided to sell them. Not having either business ability or shrewdness, she sold nine of them for $40 cash and the balance $50 monthly. This was ridiculous as the income from the nine netted more than $100 per month. It was giving them away.

The purchaser came on Sunday to close the deal. I handed him back his $40. He refused to take it. I refused to hear any talk. I told him plainly he had taken advantage of Emily's ignorance of business and to take his $40 and leave. He did.

Several months later I sold all the apartments for Emily for $500 cash, and the balance on chattel mortgage of $125 monthly, plus interest. But this time I was in debt to her for our living expenses, as all my funds were in the magazine.

Because of my help in making the sale Emily volunteered to give me the use of that $500 and also $500 more of the instalments. This I accepted. It proved the turning point. The magazine began to take hold and make money.

I was heavily in debt by this time, but with the magazine making money at last I began to pay off my debts.

Emily took a position with the concern and received $20 per week. We lived at 6444 and I paid her mother rent for both of us. Later I incorporated the business and gave Emily $1,400 worth of stock in the corporation. This was *not* in payment of the $1,000 I owed her, but was simply a gift.

Since the magazine took up so much of my time, I worked late into every night doing almost all the work myself, and saw little of Emily except at the office, usually arriving home after midnight every night.

My deep knowledge of Chicago soon was in demand before luncheon clubs, real-estate firms, and others interested in Chicago and its future. I was a fairly interesting lecturer and became proficient in this subject, being called upon to make an address almost every night in the week.

This added to my income, and, instead of putting it into my pocket, I put it into the business, paying off debts and increasing the magazine's sphere of influence. My income for my lectures was as large, if not larger, than my personal income from the publication, and almost all of it went to build up the *Greater Chicago Magazine*.

Being publisher and editor of the magazine, I received many free tickets and invitations to political, social and business dinners and affairs. Since I was on the road to success and social honor, Emily began to demand that I marry her. Her demands became so alarming that I left her home at 6444 and went to live at the Morrison Hotel. This move on my part caused the break between us that was to widen still more. I had been paying her back on the installment plan and had paid her about $500 at this time.

Finally one day in August, 1926, she came down to my room at the hotel, accompanied by her sister, and demanded that I marry her that day. I refused very pointedly. She then gave me the choice of either marrying her then and there or exposure of my escape from Georgia and all it entailed.

This was a bitter pill to me. It was only 8 o'clock. I had important business engagements to keep; deals which I had worked on for months were to be decided that day. She knew this. Besides my business affairs were in such a shape that, although the magazine had a standing and was worth considerable money, I couldn't raise much cash, if I decided to refuse her demands and pull out.

What could I do? What should I do? She knew my secret. My God! Must that ghost of the past always rise up before me; would it haunt me the rest of my days? Time was pressing and I needed a clear head for the day's activities. I pleaded, I begged, for time, for anything but exposure or marriage. But she was adamant.

I then asked her how she thought a marriage ceremony would change me or alter my opinion of her, or my conduct toward her? Would I not be the same man after the ceremony as I was now. Could or would I ever love her after being browbeaten into a marriage with her?

Argument, logic, common sense, nothing moved her. Marriage was what she wanted.

I was desperate, mad, clear through to the bone, but I kept my self-control. I didn't love any woman, perhaps never would. I'd marry her to get rid of her and maybe the future would show me a way out of it all. So that August morning in 1926 I was led to the altar.

CHAPTER IX

Success, Romance and—Betrayal

THREE YEARS rolled by. *The Greater Chicago Magazine* grew and expanded. It became a force in the civic affairs of Chicago. And I, the founder, became prominent and successful. I made many friends. I believe I was respected and honored by thousands. I delivered an average of five lectures each week during this period. An average of at least one hundred persons attended each lecture.

My message always was one of inspiration, achievement and courage, both to face and master the problems and difficulties of life. Always I pointed out the great opportunity Chicago presented to the industrious, courageous, and honest thinker and worker.

By this time it had become general knowledge that Burns's word was his bond. My credit was excellent. Banks cheerfully lent me money, which was always repaid on time. Concerns in the printing industry were eager to get my business and extend credit. I became a member of the Chicago Association of Commerce and also of the Chicago Real Estate Board.

I stood for clean politics and clean business. I supported every worthwhile civic achievement, cultural, charitable, commercial, and industrial. I helped sponsor the World Fair movement, supported it fearlessly and lectured for it often and without compensation of any kind.

In the light of subsequent events, let me bring out these self-evident truths.

The record I made in Chicago, the friends I acquired—and remember, I started as an unknown laborer and every step up was self-made—are overwhelming and convincing proof that I did live a clean, honest, wholesome and creative life, and as such was both an honor and an asset to Chicago.

And yet, there were those, so saturated with prejudice, jealousy and hatred, as to deliberately lie and slander me by saying I was and still am a menace to society!

Anyone, reading this, can readily see the dishonesty and ferociousness that some "holier than thou" officials will go to in an effort to build up a case against a man because he once escaped from a prison.

My record of seven years of honest and industrious effort, wherein I gained an honored and creative place in society, was systematically and dishonestly attacked and belittled to provide an excuse for the wreaking of vengeance. Society had nothing to lose and everything to gain if I continued as publisher and editor of the *Greater Chicago Magazine*. But the jealousy of Emily Del Pino Pacheo Burns, and the brutal, uncompromising, vengeance of Georgian officials, caused the ruthless destruction of my business and the cruel subversion of a man who had tried and succeeded in going straight.

With success and prosperity, I had more leisure and a larger viewpoint. Success itself was an empty shell. I had missed a great force in my life. That force was love—a real home, children, a happy family life. Women began to interest me more. I had met and become acquainted with hundreds during my lectures and social engagements but always there was something lacking.

I believed in love then, and I believe in love now. Love is a mighty force—one of the greatest forces in human life and society. I began to look for love to share my success.

By this time Emily had become but an individual to me. My feeling toward her was brotherly, tolerant of her many underhanded acts, tolerant of her bitter remarks to me, and also pity for her. She had tried desperately and unfairly to win my heart, and she had failed. Frankly I told her so. True, legally I was her husband, but morally I was not.

Was it my fault that I did not love her? Can an individual will himself to love another, or is love some great consuming power—the highest pinnacle of human feeling and emotion—something both holy and divine? I take the latter view. Love is some spontaneous overwhelming force—something above and beyond the power of mortal man to will or control. And, mark you well, love knows when it is reciprocated or when it is unrequited.

Emily's fierce determination to possess me, even when she knew deep in her heart that her love was unrequited, will always be a great mystery to me, as I often told her.

In the fall of 1928 Emily did not show up at the office for two days. Although we both lived at the same house, we had drifted so far apart that we had separate rooms and rarely saw each other except at the office. I called up her mother and was told that Emily was in the South Shore Hospital. I went there that afternoon to see her. Not love, mind you, but a sense of fairness, of justice, of mercy, prompted me, for if I could help her, I most certainly would.

I found her in the cheapest ward—in very bad shape—in fact dying from a major operation for rupture. If I had been wicked, a menace to society, a criminal, I would have left her to die. My secret would have been safe, and I would have been free from a tigerish, selfish, nagging woman who made life miserable for me. At this time, November, 1928, I had paid her back every penny that was due her, and a great deal more. In fact, she had received almost $9,000 from me during and up to this time.

And when I looked at her in the hospital that fall afternoon, and saw her dying in a cheap ward, temptation came to me. I wanted to let her die and thus assure my own safety.

But, I had come up through life to the position I now held by being scrupulously honest. In all my life I had never wilfully harmed or injured anyone. No! I would show this stubborn woman I was a real man—that I was honest to the core—that I had character—that I was what all the world thought I was.

I immediately had her placed in one of the best private rooms in the hospital. The room itself cost me six dollars a day. I ordered two trained nurses, day and night. They cost me fourteen dollars a day and twenty dollars a week for their board. I ordered a specialist. I visited her every day—brought flowers and fruits—and by prompt action on my part and the care I ordered and paid for, saved her life.

She remained in the hospital until December 24, 1928, and although not quite well, she was able to be removed to her home. The expense at the hospital was $997.50, all of which I paid.

And yet, she started an argument with me that very day—Christmas Eve—because I didn't love her. And this, in face of the fact that, knowing she would be confined at home for quite a while, I had purchased and installed a beautiful radio as a Christmas gift, and also had given her an additional $50 bill.

Of course I didn't love her. I knew it, and she knew it. But because I didn't love her was no reason for not wanting to see her happy. Yet in spite of all my efforts, she flew into a violent rage because I didn't love her, and because I was going to visit my dear old mother and brothers and sisters over the Christmas holidays and leave my sick wife to take care of herself.

That was the last straw. Come what would, I was through with Emily. From then on I decided to ignore her completely, and began to take steps to secure a divorce.

In February, 1929, I met Lillian Salo. Fate plays many tricks on us all. It was by an act of chance I met her. This is how it happened.

Whenever my day's work was done, I used to turn my steps toward 6444 Ingleside Avenue. I hated myself for doing it, for that house only meant mental torture to me. No matter what time I came in, Emily was sure to wait for me to pour out a torrent of abuse. She had given me her body, her love, her money, her help—I was successful now and I was turning her down! What did it matter if I patiently explained to her that I didn't love her and never did or would. What did she want—money—freedom—a divorce—what? I offered her anything I could or had to give. But all she wanted was my love—something I had not the power to give. But she couldn't see it.

I had tried living in hotels, but always she would come and cause a scene, and the result would be that I would return to 6444. And now my heart was heavy and it was sheer will power that dragged my weary, unwilling feet to walk into that house night after night. I got into the habit of never coming in until after midnight, so as to give her as little chance to quarrel as possible.

If I were free an evening, I never went home, but sought relief somewhere in the places of amusement and recreation that the city offered.

And so, one evening in February, I had finished a lecture at 9 P.M. I was tired, but I wouldn't go home. Where could I go? Some place to get the much needed mental and physical relaxation I craved, some place of clean and wholesome amusement. I wandered aimlessly around. I had seen most of the current movies—I didn't drink—so I unconsciously entered a dance hall. And there I met Lillian Salo! Simply the hand of Destiny playing its cards and weaving the pattern of my life.

There were over one hundred women and girls there. Why did my eyes fall on that particular girl? Why did I become electrified at the sight of her? What unseen magnetic power pulled me toward her? I was mystified—I was thrilled—something had happened to me—something I could not fathom or explain—something I enjoyed and followed fearlessly.

I spoke to her—asked her to dance. She accepted. I danced with her once, twice, three times—all that night I danced with her. To me there were only two people in that hall—she and I. Something in her face thrilled me. I studied it—clean, honest, beautiful—to me an angel's face. I made an appointment with her for the next night.

We met, went out to supper, exchanged confidences, and became acquainted, and then, in the weeks that followed, we fell in love with each other.

Love! That grand, majestic, powerful force in life. Have you ever experienced deep, real, honest love? I—in love! I couldn't realize it or believe it. And yet, the world seemed brighter, happier, gayer. Places that seemed dark and ugly appeared bright and clear. I walked with a lighter step. Inspiration and enthusiasm welled up within me. The trees and grass in the parks seemed more green and more beautiful. The birds sang more sweetly. Life had a new, a deeper, a greater and a grander meaning. Love! A force that can change a squalid hut into a king's palace. Love! Love! Not unrequited love—but deep physical and mental exhilaration and admiration—shared by both.

Lillian was a music student, with a desire to become a great violinist. She had come from a poor family in Minneapolis to the great musical center, Chicago. Alone and unafraid she came. She worked in a restaurant as a waitress and studied music at night. I took her to one of the ablest violinists in Chicago, and arranged for her lessons. I told her of Emily and of my miserable life with her, and promised to marry Lillian as soon as I got a divorce.

I asked Emily to get a divorce. She said she would. Weeks went by, but she made no move. I asked again why she had not made some effort to get a divorce, and again she promised—but did nothing.

From early in February until March 27, Lillian and I met every night. We had supper together, enjoyed each other's company, and discussed our future.

Emily had made no move toward a divorce. We decided to give her cause, and to get her to act. Lillian and I decided on March 27 to take an apartment and live together. I was to tell Emily and to get her to make some move to free me.

On the morning of March 28, I called Emily into my private office and said to her:

"Emily, I want to be fair with you. I want you to know that at last the inevitable has happened. I have fallen in love with a beautiful, talented young woman. She loves me too. We want to get married. Our attraction and marriage is based on real love. Emily, this means happiness to me—perhaps fatherhood—a real, happy home—my one chance in life for real happiness. I know you have been unhappy—but please don't make me suffer also. I want you to get a divorce—I will pay the attorney's fee and I will give you twenty-five dollars a week alimony. You have a stock ownership in this business that will increase in value as the business increases. I want to be friendly with you, to remain friends. We can visit each other occasionally, and Lillian, whom you have never met, will welcome you in our new home. I have explained everything to her and she promises to be kind and tolerant toward you.

"Emily, I plead with you—I beseech you to play fair and I promise you that I will always provide for you in a financial way as long as you live. All I ask is a divorce and the silence you promised.

"This plan of mine, I think, is fair and honest, and manly. However, I want you to consider that any other action on your part will spell ruin for us all. I will face any difficulties, rather than give Lillian up; this I will never do. If you expose me I will fight to the last. If you expose me, you will never get another penny out of me or the business, and even then you will gain nothing. If I am sent back to prison, Lillian will wait for me, and we'll be married anyhow.

"You have nothing to gain by being mean or cruel, and all to gain by being sensible and just. Promise me now, on your rosary beads, on your sacred word of honor to me and to God, that you will help me, and not betray me."

And Emily promised—there in my private office on March 28—on the rosary beads of her religion—on her sacred honor, to God and the Virgin Mary of her faith, to get a divorce and *not* to expose me.

A day or two later she walked into the office like a wild woman. Without waiting to be announced, she rushed into my private inner office, and leaving the door open, shrieked at the top of her voice, "God damn you! I'm going to destroy you, or kill you! I'm going to tear you down to the same place you were in when you first met me! You have used my body, you have used my money, you have lived protected in my home, and you have become successful and on the way to wealth—and now you kick me out like a dirty dog! I tell you, I will destroy you or kill you!"

48

The whole office force heard this tirade and was astonished, and I was speechless with indignation and astonishment—and I lost my head. Instead of attempting to be diplomatic and smooth the matter over, I got angry and replied: "There's the telephone" (pointing to a phone on my desk) "expose me if you wish! Call the police now. I won't run away, but will fight you to the finish, as I never mistreated you; but I won't allow you to come between Lillian and me."

Our loud remarks caused several of the employees to interfere and Merle MacBain, my editor, and Wyndham Chant, advertising manager, stepped into my inner office, closed the door, and acted as peace-makers between Emily and me. The result of the peace conference was that Emily retracted her statements, agreed once more to go ahead with her divorce action, faithfully promising before these two witnesses that she would keep my secret and accept a weekly alimony of twenty-five dollars.

But on March 28, 1929, at the Jackson Park Post Office, at 7 P.M., was mailed her first letter to Georgia, notifying the prison authorities of my whereabouts.

CHAPTER X

The Heavy Hand Of Unfeeling Law

L OVE! WHAT a wonderful thing it is. How it can change a drab
existence to a life of wonder. Every hour becomes a joy, a blessing.
The dreams and distant hopes of years, at last come true.

We planned a home. I bought a piece of property at
Desplaines, Illinois; a suburb near the northern part of Chicago. We
selected the plans for the bungalow. We planned the interior, the
decorations, etc. Life for us was one continuous and glorious romance.
Perhaps we would have our little spats—in time they might come—but our
love was real love—not just some passing fancy or purely physical
attraction.

Success, Love, Romance, Happiness, Wealth, and a rosy future, were
mine at last! What a long uphill battle I had fought! From a chain-gang
slave to the pinnacle of real achievement. Built day by day, brick by brick,
step by step, by honest, untiring effort. Does honesty pay? Why of course
it does! Had I not acquired all of this by honesty, adherence to ideals; by
courage and real worth of character? Surely organized society could not
overlook this hard-won and deserved victory over so many obstacles and
not see that the man behind it all was now a man, tested by life's bitter
experiences and found to be of pure metal.

Some twenty-four hundred years ago Confucius said, "It is better to
fall, and rise again, than never to have fallen."

There followed two months of a wonderful existence with Lillian. Now
in the evenings when the strife of the day was over, I went home early.
She sang to me and played for me on her violin. Happy—just sheer
happiness—like two robins in the woods. When I went to lecture, she
accompanied me, and seeing her sitting in the audience, I rose to new
heights of power and eloquence. What an ideal existence! Paradise had at
last come down to earth—to me.

And Emily had secured a lawyer, one Cecil Ericksen. I was served with
a subpoena to appear in court on a divorce action. Before appearing in
court I had a conference with Emily and Ericksen. It related to his fees and

51

Emily's alimony. I offered $100 for fees, and $25 a week alimony. This they refused. Emily wanted $50 a week. Ericksen wanted a fee of $250. This I refused. We could reach no agreement. We agreed to let the court decide.

The day before our appearance in court, I was served with another paper. The action was altered from divorce to separation.

We appeared in court before Judge Gemmil of the Domestic Relations Branch. He criticized Ericksen for filing two actions, and postponed the case until Emily and her lawyer could decide what they wanted, a divorce or separation.

Ericksen spoke of fees and temporary alimony. The Judge heard their arguments and then asked me my side. I told him the story. The Judge set the fees at $50 and the alimony at $ 15 per week, and postponed the case.

Needless to say, the Judge's decision enraged and inflamed both Emily and her lawyer, and they threatened me with dire consequences. Never realizing that Emily would betray me, I laughed off their threats.

In the following week, Emily started two civil suits against me, one for $1,000 and another for $1,500. I engaged a friend of mine, Attorney Morris I. Kaplan, to defend me in those suits.

These pending legal actions were burdensome and troublesome, but I discarded them each evening as one takes off an office coat, when I went home to Lillian and our love nest.

It was now May 22, about 10 A.M. I was in conference with my editor and right-hand man, Merle MacBain.

MacBain had started to work for me three years before at $12 a week. He came to the office and begged for a job. He had heard me lecture and wanted to associate himself with me. I had no job available, but was impressed by his earnestness and manner, and created one for him. He proved his worth. He learned quickly and had become indispensable. He was now editor, a stockholder and a director. The stock was given to him from my holding gratis, in recognition of his interest, loyalty and ability.

On the morning of May 22, we were having a conference. The switchboard operator interrupted with the information that two men were waiting to see me. They had no prior appointment. I told her if they cared to wait until I was through, I would see them. The conference took about forty-five minutes. MacBain left the office and the two men entered. They closed the door, and, like a flash, one pulled a gun while the other one displayed a shield. They were detectives. They frisked me for weapons, opened the drawers of my desk, sent me into a corner—and then they read a letter to me.

That letter was from the prison authorities of Georgia!

Realizing what I was up against, I tried to get a grip on myself.

"Are you the man referred to in this letter?" one of them asked me.

I was stupefied. My head was reeling, but I tried not to show my agitation. In that one moment seven long years of toil and struggle, my hopes, my plans for the future—all began to crumble around me.

I looked up at them. I was helpless to cover the turmoil and fears that were tearing at my heart.

What could I say?

CHAPTER XI

In the Coils of Legal Red Tape

WAS I the man referred to in this letter?

"Yes," I replied. I was stupefied, my head was reeling.

Quickly they saw I was not a criminal. They were very much surprised and sympathized with me. I called in MacBain—explained the situation briefly to him, told him he would have to carry on. I called up Lillian—told her what I could in a short telephone conversation. I signed a batch of blank checks for MacBain to carry on with. And then I left with the officers.

I was locked up in the new State Street Police Headquarters with the riff-raff of the underworld.

While I was in jail, MacBain saw Attorney Kaplan and they started some plan for my release.

By 1 o'clock, Lillian finally located me. She was in tears. We talked through iron bars. She promised me her loyalty and love. She would wait for me.

The police spoke to me about extradition—I signed a waiver—and told them I'd go back. If Georgia was so vicious and cruel as to wreak its brutal vengeance on me now, I'd go back and take my medicine. Perhaps when they heard my story they'd see the injustice and let me go. Two officials from Georgia wired that they were on the way. So eager for their prey!

By 2 o'clock my friends were coming to see me. All kinds of plans were in the making. I explained that I would go back and try to find mercy and justice, if there were any in Georgia.

By 3 o'clock I was surrounded by reporters. As yet, nothing had appeared in the newspapers. I refused to make any statement. They insisted. They wouldn't take no for an answer. Someone told them I was a World War veteran. Finally, to get rid of them, I answered questions and gave them some facts. In an hour the papers were on the street with screaming headlines.

At 5 o'clock, Attorney Kaplan, accompanied by Attorney Cameron Latter, came to see me. Mr. Latter was a stranger to me. He promised that for $1,000 he would prevent extradition, and also told me that MacBain had already paid him $350 on account.

That was really news to me. I told him to go ahead. All that evening and far into the night friends—both wealthy and poor—were constantly coming in. It seemed everybody in Chicago was out to help me.

A certain high police official called me into his office. By now I was an honored prisoner. A celebrity. Everything was done for my comfort. I was treated with deference and respect. I had a talk with this official. He is a fine, able man—honest and efficient. A type of police officer that is far too scarce.

Our conversation was about as follows:

"Sit down, Burns, and make yourself at home," indicating a chair. "There are a lot of prominent people interested in your case, and it seems a pity to send you back to the chain gang. As far as I am concerned, if it is left up to me, you will never go back. I received word that two officers from Georgia are *en route* here. As long as you are in my custody, they will never get you.

"I suppose your friends are planning some legal move to defeat extradition, but if you listen to me I can fix it so you will never have to go back.

"There are a lot of unsolved murders here, as you know. I can request that you be held as a suspect in one of these cases. Naturally, you are innocent and can prove a perfect defense—but the idea is—each time the case would come up I will ask for a postponement and so drag it out for several years, and thus defeat your return to Georgia. Think this over, Burns, as I am your friend and can't see why Georgia wants you to go back after making good here. The whole thing is ridiculous."

I thanked him, and being very curious as to who and what caused my exposure, I asked:

"Do you know how Georgia notified you of my location?"

"Yes!" he answered. "I'll tell you about that. Here is an anonymous letter (handing me the letter) mailed on March twenty-eighth, nineteen twenty-nine, postmarked seven P.M., Jackson Park Station, Chicago, informing them (the Georgia officials) of your location."

I noticed at once that the letter was written by Emily. It was her handwriting.

"The Georgia authorities wrote me, enclosing this letter, and requesting me to make the arrest. I sent a man down to your office, he looked the place over, made a few inquiries about you and reported to me. He said, 'Chief, there must be some mistake here. This bird is publisher and editor of the *Greater Chicago Magazine*—a respected citizen—a member of the Chicago Association of Commerce and other civic organizations, and has been in business five years. There's something phoney here. He can't be the man.'

"After getting this report, I made a thorough examination and decided the Georgia authorities were wrong.

"About three weeks later I got another letter from Georgia, presenting their information again, and asking why no action had been taken on their tip, as you were positively the man. I wrote back, saying that their information was wrong or that someone was kidding them. That was five weeks ago. Yesterday I got a call from Swanson's office (the State Attorney), requesting my office to arrest you at once, as the State's Attorney's office was positive you were an escaped convict. I had to act and here you are."

"How did Swanson's office get the information?" I again asked.

"Well, that puzzled me, too," the official replied, "but it seems the party who turned you up, seeing no results from her letters to Georgia, went to Swanson's office a couple of days ago and put in the 'rap' there. Swanson's office got in touch with Georgia and then demanded that I bring you in. Who in hell is so anxious to send you back?"

"My wife," I replied. "That first letter is in her handwriting and she lived in Jackson Park."

"Well, it is a damned shame, Burns, but if you let me handle this you can stay in Chicago as long as I have anything to say about it. Take it easy now and have a talk with this reporter from the *Trib*, and I guess, with all your friends, you will get out of it yet."

I retired to another room with the reporter and answered questions and gave out my first real interview.

The next morning Cameron Latter, my attorney, filed a petition for a writ of habeas corpus heard before Judge David of the Supreme Court.

Court opened at 10 A.M. I was simply dumbfounded at the immense throng that appeared for the hearing. The courtroom was packed to the doors and the crowd overflowed into the corridors outside. Everywhere, on every side, friends, strangers, everybody, was anxious and willing to help. A spontaneous feeling of the injustice that would be done if I were returned, was apparent on every side.

The hearing began with the usual formalities. I was represented by Messrs. Kaplan and Latter. Ex-Judge Q. Chott, Assistant State's Attorney, represented the State of Illinois and also, in an *ex-officio* capacity, the State of Georgia. County Commissioner Redwine and a county officer, both of Campbell County, Georgia, were also there, ready to take me back.

After the preliminaries were over, Judge David spoke at great length. I will not record here all he said, for most of it was about the legal technicalities involved. He did say the following, however:

"Georgia—the Great State of Georgia—the home and birthplace of that vicious organization, the Ku Klux Klan. Where they sell the water of the Chattahochee River at five dollars per gallon to baptize the ignorant and illiterate, that they may be initiated into the wonders of the Klan, and so continue their holy and Christian persecution of the Jew, the Catholic, and the Negro; and become acquainted with the fine art of lynching and midnight beatings and terrorism.

"The purpose of the law is for protection of society and *not* for vengeance. It seems to me that Georgia in this case does not want justice but vengeance. Personally, I cannot see anything in this most peculiar situation but vengeance. Society has nothing to gain by returning this man to a brutal prison, neither has it anything to fear if he continues to remain free."

He next questioned the officials from Georgia about conditions and treatment of prisoners. Upon receiving replies regarding conditions, he said:

"It is brutal and cruel and inhuman to work a prisoner in stripes and in chains upon the public roads, exposed to the view of the populace and to be pointed out as a felon." As the officials from Georgia had no official papers for my extradition, he informed them that if they ever expected to get me they would have to present the proper papers, properly signed by both the Governor of Georgia and Governor Emmerson of Illinois.

The next question that came up was as to my status during the continuation of the hearing, as it was apparent that no decision would be reached that day. Attorney Latter requested that I be admitted to bail.

This was opposed by ex-Judge Chott and also by the officials from Georgia. The matter of bail for an escaped convict became involved in a legal discussion between the lawyers present, and the Judge reserved his decision. However, he decided that I should be released from police custody, and ordered that I be placed in the care of the County Sheriff. The police officers present had no objection to this decision and court was adjourned until the following morning. A deputy sheriff was assigned to take me to the county jail.

The Sheriff was a friend of mine and instead of taking me to the county jail, he assigned a deputy to me, with the understanding that I could go and come as I pleased, providing I paid the expenses of the deputy sheriff who was to accompany me wherever I went.

The following morning at the opening of court, still greater crowds were in the courtroom and the corridors. Also by this time the story had crashed the front pages of all the important dailies in America, and great interest was aroused throughout the country. The hearing opened and again the question of bail was brought up, and again strenuously opposed by the State's Attorney's office and the officials of Georgia. Friends of mine were in court and publicly announced that, if necessary, they would put up five million dollars for bond.

Judge David said that, as the State of Illinois was not interested in the case, he would not accept a bond schedule. He would, however, admit me to bail on a cash bond of $5,000, which money was to be deposited with the clerk of his court and placed in the court safe. If I should jump bail, this $5,000 was to be turned over to the State of Georgia. This proposition was also strenuously opposed by ex-Judge Chott of the State Attorney's office. The officials of Georgia, now completely confused and bewildered by the open feeling of resentment heard on all sides against their efforts, were unable to make any comment on the subject of bond.

Immediately on hearing the Judge's decision on cash bond, half a dozen of my business associates rushed out of the courtroom to get the money. The first one back was Mr. C. C. Niles, Vice-President of H. O. Stone & Company, the oldest firm in Chicago—ninety-three years in business in the city. He presented a certified check to Judge David, which was accepted, and I was released on bond. The move of releasing me on bond was vigorously opposed by Judge Chott and comment on his objection was heard on every side. It caused Judge David to ask him in open court why he was so opposed to releasing me on bond. Judge Chott replied that my wife had made serious charges against me, accusing me of violating the laws of Illinois. This accusation startled the Judge and everyone in the courtroom. Judge David then replied:

"This man can go back to Georgia a hundred years from now, if necessary, but, if the State Attorney's office of Cook County has evidence of any crimes committed by him, it is the duty of the State Attorney's office to indict him and try him here *before* he returns to Georgia."

As Judge David spoke these words a hush fell over the courtroom. It was in effect an ultimatum.

What were those who were working against me going to do about it?

Would they accept the challenge?

"Judge Chott, how much time do you think your office would require to make this investigation?" Judge David asked.

Judge Chott replied: "Your Honor—at least, about ten. days."

Judge David, answering said: "I will give you two weeks. Court will be adjourned, and in two weeks from today, when this hearing shall be resumed, I, personally want to hear the result of the investigation of these accusations."

CHAPTER XII

The Fight against Extradition

RETURNING TO my office after this hearing at about one o'clock in the afternoon, I found the place in utmost confusion. Friends, business associates, strangers, newspapermen and photographers were all awaiting my arrival from Court.

Everybody wanted to know what a Georgia chain gang was like. Everybody wanted to know how I had escaped. The newspapermen wanted a story. The photographers wanted pictures. Business associates wanted to know how they could help or aid me in defeating extradition. Everybody was sure, positive, certain that I would never have to go back to the chain gang. It was ridiculous, it was unthinkable, they said.

Amazed by this extraordinary feeling in my behalf, I was deeply affected, as it was inconceivable to me that I had so many staunch and sincere friends.

The business had to go on, however, so I got rid of the newspapermen and photographers without giving any interviews at this time and went into conference with several business associates present to lay plans for defeating the extradition warrant that by this time was on the way from Georgia.

So many plans were formed that I really don't know myself what was actually done. I do know, however, that Mr. William Eichenbaum, Vice-President of the Metropolitan Realty Company, and the Reverend Mr. F. E. Bennett, of Forest Park, chartered an airplane with the expectation of getting an interview on my behalf with Governor Hardman of Georgia.

They were at the airport ready to take off immediately upon receiving his reply. However, the day previous, newspaper correspondents had interviewed the Governor of Georgia, relative to my case, and had sent the following wire to Chicago papers:

"There is nothing I can do until Burns has been returned to prison in Georgia. Consequently, it will be useless for me to see your delegation and waste your time and mine.

"Until Burns is back in prison, I will not entertain any clemency plea until the matter has been handled according to our routine, first by the Prison Commission, and then by me.

"Of course, I cannot and will not say what my course then will be. I will be governed entirely by the record, as presented, and will be guided by the recommendations of the Prison Commission.

"I can see no reason why I should depart from my established custom and the established custom of all Georgia's governors of recent years."

Upon receiving this information we decided to center our efforts with Governor Emmerson of Illinois. Immediately a committee was formed and hundreds of letters and telegrams were sent to Governor Emmerson by prominent Chicagoans requesting that he refuse to honor the extradition warrant when it arrived from Georgia.

Another committee was formed by a group of prominent business men under the name of "The Burns Citizens Committee." This committee was headed by Mr. Axel Lonnquist, with temporary offices at his place of business at 111 West Washington Street.

Letters describing my case and petition forms asking for a great public roll of signatures were prepared and distributed. The Committee's letter read as follows:

"Once having experienced penal servitude marks many men for perpetual membership in the ranks of the enemies of society. Not so in the case of Robert E. Burns.

"He chose the straight and narrow path, persevered therein and won to real success and honor. He became a member of the Chicago Association of Commerce, the Chicago Real Estate Board and many other prominent civic bodies of the city. He advanced the welfare of numerous worthy civic, cultural, charitable and religious causes through the medium of his publication, an organ of municipal growth and progress. He was one of the first to work toward the development of plans for the second Chicago World's Fair.

"A writer of inspirational poetry and an able speaker, Mr. Burns was in constant demand as a lecturer before large real-estate and civic organizations. Having reconstructed his own life, he helped many another to get a new grip and to win success.

"Today, he is known and respected by thousands of Chicagoans who have come in contact with him in the course of their business life. He is regarded as a genuine civic asset to Chicago.

"Robert E. Burns has been scarred by life, both in battle for his country on foreign fields and during the trying transition to peace-time which brought him into difficulties.

"If correction and reconstruction be the purpose of prisons, then surely Robert E. Burns is an example of a man in whom this purpose has been amply fulfilled. He has worked out his own salvation, and is today a respected, worthy and creative member of society.

"Will you help him to remain so?

BURNS CITIZEN COMMITTEE.

In response to the many telegrams and letters that he received in my behalf Governor Emmerson granted a hearing to my attorneys and friends before making his decision in the matter. This hearing was held in Springfield, Illinois, sometime early in June. Before the hearing took place, however, newspapermen had interviewed my wife. Her rage and fury had now reached the boiling point, and in her overwhelming desire to injure me in some way, she gave out an interview accusing me of bigamy and of embezzlement. I can account for this in no other way except to say that the unexpected public sympathy my case had aroused appalled her, and she began to fear that she would not have her expected revenge.

Besides saying that I was guilty of these offenses, she also attacked my war record by asserting that I had not been a soldier with the A. E. F. This last statement caused a lot of confusion and doubt, as my army discharge was in possession of my mother at Pittsfield, Massachusetts.

My brother, the Reverend Vincent G. Burns, of Palisade, New Jersey, arrived in Chicago to accompany me to the hearing before Governor Emmerson at Springfield.

In the light of subsequent events, especially at my two hearings before the Prison Board in Georgia, and other happenings which I will relate, there was always a vague, indistinct and elusive power that seemed to work against me continually. What or who this power was I do not know. But this I do know, that the only known enemy I had was my wife and she could never, single-handed and alone, have created and put into action the force that was used to obstruct my parole.

Some other force was there. In searching my mind for an explanation, I was at a complete loss to account for it.

Thus it became apparent that besides having a host of friends who were straining every effort to save me from going back to prison, it is possible that I had powerful forces lined up against me.

By the time the two weeks were up, and the hearing again resumed before Judge David in Superior Court, the case had become complicated by the new accusations of my wife, which had now become public, and the crosscurrent of political factors.

On the morning the hearing was resumed, there was not such a great crowd in the courtroom, but the interest was still at high tension. After the formalities of opening court were over, Judge David again pointedly asked Assistant State's Attorney Chott if the State's Attorney's office had made investigation of my wife's accusations, and if there was any basis for legal action against me in the State of Illinois.

Judge Chott replied by saying that his office had investigated the charges, and that they were insufficient on which to base any criminal action against me. The Judge then postponed the case until after the hearing on the extradition proceeding? before Governor Emmerson of Springfield.

A few days later, accompanied by my attorneys, Messrs. Kaplan and Latter, and my brother and a few friends, I went to Springfield. The hearing was held before a member of Governor Emmerson's legislative committee, who promised us that he would submit all the facts to the Governor and that we would receive a decision in a day or so.

Two days later, my attorneys were notified that although Governor Emmerson was legally bound to recognize Georgia's right to my return, and that he had signed the extradition papers, he did so reluctantly.

After hearing Governor Emmerson's verdict, I was very much depressed, and the nightmare of the possibility of six more years on a chain gang rose before me. Between the time of my arrest on May 22 and up until the time Governor Emmerson signed the papers, the spontaneous efforts of my friends had led me to have high hopes of holding a respected position in society.

There I was, with everything that a man could wish for in life: business, friends, position, means and love. And now it was all crumbling away before my very eyes.

CHAPTER XIII

Back to the Horrors of the Gang

I TOOK STOCK of the situation. I was not in prison yet and there were many doors of escape still left. Rather than go back to the chain gang, I would sacrifice all but love. That was what hurt me most. If I went back, I would lose that which is the hardest thing to find in the world—a real, true love and all that it implies. Come what may, I reasoned, I would sacrifice anything but Lillian Salo.

I evolved a new plan and went into consultation with my attorneys. What were the courses open to me?

One: There was still the possibility that Judge David would dismiss me on my writ of *habeas corpus*, but that would leave me free only in the State of Illinois.

Two: There was the police official, and his plan, which now looked very encouraging.

Three: If we could get the State's Attorney's office of Illinois to indict me on the charges preferred by my wife, I was sure to be acquitted, because the charges were untrue. That would react in my favor to such an extent that a strong public sentiment would be created that would prove I was the victim of intrigue and vengeance.

Four: There was still the possibility of presenting my case through the proper channels to the officials of Georgia, and once they knew the truth, they would perhaps let me go free.

Five: The world is a large place. There are many countries, and the sun shines just as bright in Australia or in South Africa as it does in Chicago. In short, to take Lillian Salo with me and run away to some foreign country and start life anew.

These were the five doors of escape. Which one should I use? In discussing the case with my lawyers, they approved of only the first and fourth methods. They assured me that Judge David would not dismiss my writ and that, at their request, would continue to postpone decision on the *habeas corpus* hearing indefinitely, even continuing the case for years, if necessary.

This was my attorneys' plan at this stage, but that plan I would not, and could not, accept because it would confine my person within the borders of Illinois and it would place upon me an innuendo that could not be readily shaken off, and I would still have no status or standing but that of a fugitive and an escaped convict. This, you can readily see, would hamper the operation of my business.

I was paying for legal advice and here was a problem that I could not solve so I decided to try the fourth method, of which my legal advisers also approved. This plan was further accentuated by letters that we had received from several attorneys in Atlanta, offering and guaranteeing to secure my parole.

Attorney John E. Echols of Atlanta, who defended me at the time I was convicted, wrote a lengthy letter to me stating that, if I would return voluntarily to Georgia, he would secure an immediate parole or pardon for me in view of the fact that there was an immense sentiment in Georgia in my favor.

I instructed Attorney Latter to go to Atlanta, see the Prison Commission if possible, secure the most able and responsible lawyer in the State and to find out definitely what I could expect if I returned voluntarily. Mr. Latter left for Atlanta the next day.

After seven days in Atlanta, Mr. Latter called me on the long distance wire. He informed me that he had retained William S. Howard, ex-congressman, ex-state solicitor, executive member of the Democratic party of the State of Georgia, and the most powerful political figure and the ablest attorney in the State of Georgia.

After conferences with Attorney Howard and Attorney Echols, Mr. Latter further informed me as follows:

One: That my fate was in the hands of the Prison Commission, who recommend pardon or paroles to the Governor. They drew small salaries and were not averse to accepting gratuities to this end, as had been the custom in Georgia for many, many years.

Two: That I must return voluntarily and repay the State all the expense it had incurred it its efforts to extradite me.

Three: That I would have to go back to the chain gang from forty-five to ninety days so as to make everything look regular.

Four: I was to be sure to see that sufficient proof of my character and life for the past seven years was placed in their hands in support of their contemplated action.

Five: This would cost me $2,500, $1,000 for Mr. Howard and $500 to each of the prison commissioners.

This was indeed good news, and while the whole arrangement was purely tentative, I told him to go ahead with the deal, as I would meet the terms.

While accepting the terms presented to me from Georgia, I do not want anyone to think it was my intention to buy a parole or pardon. I believed then, as I believe now, that when you look into the facts of my case, I was entitled to either a pardon or parole on pure merit. However, having no other alternative, I accepted the proposition as Mr. Latter presented it to me.

Upon Mr. Latter's return to Chicago, I discussed the thing with him at great length, and to be certain that I was making no mistake, I went to see my friend, Mr. Hal Lytle, Vice-President of the Chicago Rapid Transit Company and also Vice-President of several other of Mr. Samuel Insull's Illinois Public Service corporations.

I laid the proposition before him and asked him if he would be so kind as to make an investigation through the immense political and financial organizations at his command, to determine if Georgia would deliver as promised. This he agreed to do and advised me to get in touch with him in a day or so in order to give him time.

Two days later, he informed me that through one of their subsidiary companies, the Georgia Light & Power Company, he had been advised that the deal would go through without a hitch.

Now, my only problem was to obtain $2,500 in cash, and also pay Mr. Latter the balance of his fee still due, which was around $650. Roughly, I would need about $3,200 in cash, which at the moment, I did not have, although my business and other possessions, real estate, etc., were worth many times this sum.

Since I had decided to accept the plan, my next step was to raise the money.

Mr. C. G. Niles, Vice-President of H. O. Stone & Company, advanced me $1,000 and took payment in the form of future advertising in my paper.

Mr. George F. Dixon, President of the George F. Dixon Company, likewise contributed $600.

Mr. Hal Lytle, Vice-President of the Chicago Rapid Transit Company, also contributed $600.

Ten or twelve other firms contributed voluntarily amounts ranging from ten to one hundred dollars. This enabled me to pay Mr. Latter the balance due him and left me approximately $2,000.

As Merle MacBain had advanced Mr. Latter $350 of the Corporation's funds on the day I was arrested, I repaid this advance to the Corporation, leaving me approximately $1,650 to apply on the $2,500 that I was to pay William Schley Howard.

While this was not the full amount agreed upon, Mr. Latter informed me that he would explain this deficiency to Mr. Howard, and that he would vouch for my payment of the balance *after* I was released, on a monthly payment plan.

Even then, when arrangements seemed to have been perfect, I had a deep unshakable intuition that all was not well, and that I was taking a long chance in going back to the chain gang, as I knew from experience that Georgia officials were very, very fickle.

Here was the first situation in my entire career where I ever acted upon the advice of others. In all my life, before and since, I rarely had accepted advice, preferring to calmly and thoroughly reason out a situation and come to a conclusion that coincided with both thought and emotion.

Somehow, I could not banish from my mind the feeling that the outcome of my voluntary return to the chain gang was very much in doubt. But, on the other hand, there was the advice of Mr. Lytle, a tremendous power in the scheme of things. There was the word of Attorney Schley Howard of Georgia, another strong political influence over the destinies of the people of Georgia. There was the payment of part of the amount requested. And last, but most convincing, was the pure merit of my cause. It looked copper-riveted. But still the hazy, indefinite, subconscious feeling persisted, whispering to my inner consciousness that there was a hitch in this carefully laid plan.

Before I had definitely established a date upon which I would return to Georgia, my deliberations were cut short by a new development.

Mr. Vivian Stanley, one of the Prison Commissioners, was on his way to Chicago. I met him at the La Salle Street Station, took him to the Atlantic Hotel and later to the office of my attorneys. We discovered that he had come to Chicago in response to a telegram from the State's Attorney's office stating that I would be delivered to him. This was a bit high-handed on the State's Attorney's part, as no decision had been reached on the hearing of my writ of *habeas corpus*.

In the five years during which I published the *Greater Chicago Magazine,* I had never entered a political campaign, preferring to remain neutral.

But when State's Attorney Swanson ran against Robert E. Crowe, who had been State's Attorney of Cook County for ten years and had built up a powerful political organization, I supported Judge Swanson with full-page editorials in the *Greater Chicago Magazine.*

Judge Swanson accomplished the unexpected and beat the machine in the primaries. In the months preceding the election I continued to support Judge Swanson fearlessly, both by editorials and by lectures. Judge Swanson's election startled Chicago.

In assisting him, the *Greater Chicago Magazine* had broken a five-year rule to keep out of politics. I had asked nothing in return and had done this purely out of a civic pride in the city of Chicago. Previous to my exposure, I believed that State's Attorney Swanson was my sincere friend.

This telegram to the Prison Commission, which Mr. Stanley showed me, convinced me that somebody had influenced Swanson. You will see later on that the State's Attorney's office of Cook County was anxious to see me returned to the Georgia chain gang.

While discussing the possibilities of my early release from the chain gang with Mr. Stanley, he informed both my attorneys and myself that if I went back voluntarily with him and repaid the State of Georgia all the expense they had incurred and got my business associates and friends to write to the Commission, that I would be back in Chicago in from forty-five to ninety days.

He further stipulated that I would be made a trusty *at once,* given certain privileges and would not be compelled to work on the public roads. I must say here that Mr. Stanley's demeanor and attitude convinced me that he was sincere and that I would be in Georgia only a short while.

I decided to return with him at once.

We arranged with Judge David to resume the hearing on the writ for the purpose of taking character testimony in the presence of Mr. Vivian Stanley, and that that testimony would be recorded by a court stenographer and placed in the hands of the Georgia Prison Commission.

In the interval, Mr. Stanley being a stranger in Chicago, and there being many wonderful things there for him to see, I arranged for his comfort and pleasure at my expense.

On the following morning, we all appeared before Judge David. Approximately seventy-five responsible and reputable business men, some of them the leading citizens of this great city, testified as to the length of time they had known me and as to my citizenship, character and moral responsibility. This testimony was heard by Mr. Vivian Stanley and was recorded by a court stenographer employed at my expense by Attorney Latter.

At the conclusion of swearing in the witness, Judge David called Assistant State's Attorney Ex-Judge Q. J. Chott before the bar. In no uncertain manner, he demanded the Ex-Judge to explain the result of the State's Attorney's office's investigation of the charges preferred by my wife.

Judge David said: "Have you made a complete investigation?"

"Yes," replied Ex-Judge Chott.

"Is there any basis for criminal action against Burns here in Illinois?" continued Judge David.

"No," was Chott's reply.

"If this man returns to Georgia voluntarily, which he is proposing to do, and after he is in prison criminal accusations are made against him, it will obstruct his chances for parole," the Judge said. "I will refuse to allow this man to return under a cloud. The State of Illinois must decide now whether it has any basis for action against him or forever remain silent."

The Judge now addressed Mr. Vivian Stanley, asking him what treatment the Georgia Prison Commission would extend to me. He was particularly anxious to know if I would be chained up and compelled to work on the roads. Mr. Stanley replied that I would not be chained and that I would not be worked on the public highways.

Instead, I would be given some clerical duties or work around the camp. It being understood by all that I was to return to Georgia voluntarily on the following morning under the conditions mentioned, the

Judge again postponed the hearing on the writ until July 3. He explained that this action was taken since something might come up between the time we left Court and the following morning, which might necessitate some unexpected change in my plans for the future.

That evening, in discussing the situation with Lillian Salo, in our apartment, I put the proposition up to her as follows:

"Lillian," I said, "I'm going back to Georgia tomorrow. You are aware of what this means. I probably will be back within forty-five to ninety days but I may not be back for six years.

"I'm going back for your sake, more than anything else. I want to clear my name and marry you as soon as I am divorced from Emily.

"I know you love me, and you know that I love you. Which course do you want me to take? Go back to Georgia and gamble on the result—or leave with you for the Pacific Coast and take a steamer to Australia to start life anew there together?"

"Elliott," she said, "under man's laws, we are unmarried, but before the eyes of God, and in the innermost feelings of our hearts, I am truly your wife. I love you, and whatever you do or wherever you go, will be agreeable to me.

"I cannot see why Georgia will not go through with its end of the deal and let you go. If anyone deserves clemency, you do. If I thought for one minute that you would have to be there six years, I would ask you for my sake, not to go back, and we would start together at once for Australia. But I am sure you will return again from Georgia in a few months."

The following morning I left the house with her. She was carrying her violin and was to take a violin lesson. She was to accompany me downtown where I was to meet Mr. Stanley. I tenderly bid her good-by at the corner of Randolph and Wells Streets, and watched her walk up the steps of the Elevated and disappear into the station.

Walking a few blocks to my attorneys' office, where I was to meet Mr. Stanley, I had a violent premonition that that was the last time I would ever see Lillian.

Alas, while the premonition did not come true as I pictured it in my mind then, it came only too true in fact, as later developments will reveal.

There were quite a number of people in Attorney Kaplan's office at 134 North La Salle Street where I was to meet Mr. Stanley. The arrangements I had made for Mr. Stanley's enjoyment of his short stay in Chicago included a visit to a famous Chicago night club.

We left for Atlanta on the morning of June 24, 1929, from the Illinois Central Station about 11 o'clock. Mr. Stanley's conversation with me that morning raised my hopes to the highest pitch.

All the way down on the long trip, we discussed my case and Mr. Stanley was positive in his statements to me that I would be back in Chicago, a free man, in ninety days.

We arrived in Atlanta about 8 o'clock in the morning and were met by a large delegation of newspapermen and Attorney Echols who took Mr. Stanley to his home in his car and myself to his office.

Mr. Echols told me that everything was all right and that I would soon have my freedom. He showed me a book containing a list of the members of the State Legislature of Georgia. He checked off a great number of them who, he claimed, were in favor of my immediate parole.

He further stated that he had made a trip to Valdosta, Georgia, and had seen Judge E. D. Thomas of the Georgia Superior Court who sentenced me. The Judge told him that he would neither approve nor disapprove of my parole, but would follow the recommendations of the Prison Commission. Mr. Echols led me to believe that he had gone to great expense, involving time and money, in my behalf, and impressed this thought on me so unctuously that I felt there was but one way to conclude the interview. I gave him a check for $100.

It so happens that Mr. Echols' offices are in the same building as the offices of Attorney Schley Howard, and as I was anxious to see Mr. Howard, Mr. Echols took me to Mr. Howard's office. After a few minutes' wait, I secured an audience with Mr. Howard. After the introduction and formalities were over, I asked Mr. Howard this question:

"Are you sure that I will be liberated in a few months?"

Mr. Howard looked at me and replied:

"As matters stand *now*, I see no reason why you should not be on your way back to Chicago in ninety days, but there is many a slip twixt the cup and the lip, and it is possible that you may have to remain incarcerated for one year. But no matter what happens, or what may develop, I can positively secure your release after twelve months."

"*Twelve months?*" I looked at him in amazement.

I was dumbfounded.

CHAPTER XIV

A Request for Money—and a Transfer

HERE WAS the strongest individual political power in Georgia, William Schley Howard, bluntly telling me that it was possible that I would have to remain in prison a year. I was frightened and discouraged, and replied:

"Do you mean to say that after coming back here voluntarily, paying my own fare, repaying the State of Georgia, and paying you your fee, and all this in the face of the merits of my reformation, it is possible I may be in prison a year?"

His answer was: "You are now in Georgia and things will have to be handled from the Georgia viewpoint."

Very much worried, I explained to him that I did not have the full fee with me, and, further, that I did not believe I should pay the full fee if I had to remain in prison a year. However, as evidence of my faith in the original agreement, I tendered him a check for $700 with the understanding that if I was liberated at the agreed time, I would arrange for payment of the balance before I left the state.

He accepted the check and the terms of payment.

About this time, Mr. Stanley arrived at the office with Mr. F. H. Redwine, Chairman of the Campbell County Commissioners. They commenced to figure up the expense to which the State of Georgia had been put in attempting to secure my extradition. Since the exact figure would entail considerable calculation, I asked them to merely estimate an approximate amount large enough to cover it.

They assured me that $350 would cover everything but the payment of the reward which they were not sure the State was going to pay. I gave Mr. Redwine a check for $350 made out to him as chairman of the Campbell County Commissioners, which was accepted.

Newspaper correspondents and photographers were clamoring for news and pictures, and were filling the office to the point of overflowing. In order to get rid of them and to carry on our transaction, I posed for several pictures. One of them was a group consisting of Stanley, Redwine and myself.

The next thing we discussed was which particular one of the 140 chain gangs in Georgia I would go to, and what my duties at the chain gang would consist of. Attorney Howard, who was formerly County Solicitor and Congressional Representative for the district which embraces Campbell County, advised me to go to the Campbell County chain gang, stating in no uncertain manner that he would see to it that I would receive fair treatment from those in charge there.

Mr. Stanley also advised me to go to this particular chain gang. Accepting their advice, I went that same afternoon, accompanied by Mr. Redwine, to the Campbell County chain gang.

It was just seven years and five days from the time that I had escaped from this particular chain gang until I returned.

I arrived at the chain gang at 4 o'clock that afternoon. Mr. Redwine introduced me to Warden Paul Phillips, who was then in charge.

Not a single prisoner, white or black, of the thirty odd prisoners here, was at this prison at the time I escaped. Also, the entire personnel of the guards had been changed.

I was assigned to the same bunk in the same pie-wagon that I had occupied when I had been here seven years previous. In fact, the only change that I could see was that there were different prisoners and guards there now.

For the sake of truth, I want to emphatically state that in my five weeks at Campbell County, I was treated intelligently, fairly and from the viewpoint that I was not a desperate criminal and was entitled to some consideration from the prison authorities.

I was made a trusty, as agreed, and was given the position of yardman. My duties were very light and consisted solely of taking care of rations, clothes, keeping a few records and reading the mail. I had come to like Warden Phillips, as he was intelligent, human and square. These five weeks at Campbell County led me to believe that the deal was going through smoothly and efficiently. I had sent to Chicago and had a special gold Masonic ring made for Warden Phillips with the inscription on the inside showing my appreciation of his treatment of me. This ring cost $65.

Could such gentle treatment be purely for the purpose of aggravating the horrors that I was to endure later?

Three weeks of separation had been too much for Lillian Salo, and she wrote me saying that she was coming to Atlanta to obtain employment there and remain in Georgia until I was free. On receiving this letter from her, I emphatically told her not to come to visit me until she had first seen my Georgia attorneys, Messrs. Howard and Echols.

I was pleasantly surprised on the fourth Sunday of my stay at Campbell County to see her. She arrived about 10 o'clock accompanied by Mr. Echols in his car. Mr. Echols told me at that time that there "was nothing to it" as I would be on my way "up the country" in a few more weeks.

Once, during the week, Attorney Howard visited me, and Lillian Salo also accompanied him to the camp. On the following Sunday, both of the attorneys paid me a visit and Lillian was again with them. At no time during these visits had I ever left the direct confines of the camp, nor was I ever outside of the direct view of a guard.

By this time I was on cordial terms with all the guards and prisoners at Campbell County chain gang. Vast crowds of curiosity seekers would come out each Sunday for the purpose of seeing me and having me pointed out to them. I had a confidential conversation about this time with one of the guards, whose name I now forget, but who for some time previous had been Clerk of the Court of Campbell County, and so was "in the know."

During this conversation, he said: "Burns, when you run out of money, you'll just make your time. All this pretence and treatment you are now receiving is simply a case of marking time until the sentiment in your behalf dies down."

This prediction came true sooner than even he had expected.

On July 29 at 5 o'clock in the evening, Attorney Echols again paid me a visit. He came to his point very abruptly and said:

"You know, Burns, the Prison Commissioners do not receive a large salary and it is customary for them to receive some gratuity when recommending a convict for parole. Your hearing is only nine days away. To be frank with you. . . ."

What he told me changed my feelings from astonishment to anger.

"I haven't got five hundred dollars with me and my personal bank account does not contain that much at this time, but if my parole hinges on paying this money I will wire to Chicago and secure the money in a few days, but I must have some positive proof that after paying this sum I will get out next month," I replied, masking my feelings as well as I could.

"I don't know how this will be regarded, but I do know the money is needed today," Echols said.

"Well," I answered, "it's utterly impossible for me to give you five hundred dollars today as I haven't it, and it would take me at least two or three days to get it."

Attorney Echols left the camp in his automobile a few minutes after 5 o'clock. It is about thirty-five miles from the camp to the offices of the Prison Commission in Atlanta—about a forty-five minute ride in an automobile.

I want the reader to remember this detail.

At 7 P.M. an eight-cylinder shiny Buick drove up to the camp. In it were two large, heavy-built men in shirt sleeves. Each one wore a bandolier supporting a large .45 caliber automatic. The younger and stouter of these men asked me where Warden Phillips was, as I was sitting in the Warden's office.

I went out and told the Warden that someone wanted to see him. After a short conversation with these men, the Warden called me over to where they were talking.

"Burns," he said, "I want you to meet Warden Hardy of the Troup County chain gang. Captain Hardy has a transfer to take you to his chain gang tonight."

Immediately the idea flashed through my mind—Echols would have arrived at the Prison Commission offices *without* the money at around 6 o'clock, making it possible for a car leaving the Prison Commission office after Echols' arrival, to reach Campbell County at about the same time at which Warden Hardy had arrived at the camp.

With this thought in mind, I immediately asked:

"Did you just come from Atlanta?"

"Yes," Warden Hardy admitted.

My heart turned to lead in my bosom, for I now realized that I would get no parole at the hearing that was to take place in nine days.

Being a convict and having no other course open but to obey the orders, I picked up my few trinkets and got in the Warden's car for my journey to Troup County, seventy-two miles from Atlanta.

On the way down, Warden Hardy said:

"Burns, you are going to a real chain gang now. We have thirty-eight mules, automatic dump wagons, scrapers, tractors, trucks and road machines, and about eighty-five convicts and twenty guards. At *my* camp, the convicts really 'chain-gang.' There is no stalling there."

"What kind of a job have you in mind for me?" I asked.

"Well," he replied, "I haven't just made up my mind yet, but after we become better acquainted and I see what kind of a prisoner you make, I can then assign you some special job, if there is any open."

"What do you think of my chances for a parole at next week's hearing?" I asked.

"Well, I don't know. There is too much publicity on your case, which the Prison Commission does not like. Still, there are so many people for you that you may not be there long. However, if it comes to pass that you should have to make these six years and you behave yourself, to my satisfaction, I will try to take care of you."

I arrived at the Troup County stockade at 9 o'clock. A few minutes later I was locked up in the bull pen with the thirty other white convicts.

CHAPTER XV

Life at the Troup County Stockade

WHEN THE great steel door closed with a bang behind the La Grange stockade all hope left me.

It was 9 o'clock on a hot July night, the year, 1929. A dim, solitary light cast dancing shadows over a large square room, divided in the middle by a row of concrete pillars. Through the flickering shadows I was able to observe the room and its contents. The walls, floor and ceiling were cold and gray. Somber and barren concrete was on every side. Several long wooden tables and benches, two large, rusted iron tubs partly filled with dirty water, and at the far end a large peculiar contraption made of wooden boards and beams, with a protruding lever, were all that it contained.

On one of the tables was a tin plate containing coarse food, already set out in anticipation of my arrival.

"So that's the Yankee that all the fuss is about," said one of the guards to an official. "He don't look so bad to me."

"He is a tricky one," answered the official, "and if he gets away I'll lose my job, and whoever is guarding him will get fired also. Those are the orders direct from Atlanta."

Having finished my cold middlings and corn pone, I was locked up for the night in the bull pen, directly above, where the rest of the convicts were already sleeping.

The La Grange stockade had the reputation of being the safest and strictest chain-gang camp of the 140-odd camps in the State.

Among its inmates were the desperate, fearless, hardened men from other camps; prisoners who had escaped and were recaptured, and those who were without friends or political aid. They were sent here for safe keeping: to prevent by every known human ingenuity their escape. It was a place shunned by everyone of Georgia's 5,000-odd felons.

As I was locked in the bull pen, a guard changed the figures on a small blackboard to read:

White prisoners	33
Black prisoners	69
Total	102

I made the thirty-third white convict in the worst chain-gang camp of them all. Someone was determined to see that I felt the full weight of the law. And—I was to be closely watched—I must never escape.

I was awakened in the middle of the night by a harsh cry.

"Everybody up, and I mean you! Everybody up, and I mean you!"

The steel barred door of the bull pen was unlocked and with two guards searching them the convicts started to file out one at a time.

"What time of night is it?" I asked of the man next to me.

"Three o'clock—time to go to work."

The convicts assembled in the mess hall, and began to eat their breakfast, which was already on the tables. Only two or three attempted to wash in the dirty water standing in the two badly rusted iron tubs. Half awake, they ate their middlings, hoe cake, sorghum and coffee in sleepy and moody silence. For the fourteen months I was at this camp breakfast never varied—it was identical for 365 days in the year.

Breakfast over, the prisoners assembled in the yard in the dark, and scrambled for positions on Ford trucks which carried us to the scene of our labors.

Just as day was breaking in the east we Commenced our endless heart-breaking toil. We began in mechanical unison and kept at it in rhythmical cadence until sundown—fifteen and a half hours of steady toil—as regular as the ticking of a clock.

In the chain gangs, human labor had been synchronized as the goose step was in the German Army. When using pickaxes, all picks hit the ground at the same time, all are raised and steadied for the next blow with uncanny mechanical precision. So it is with all work, shoveling, hammering, drilling. The convict bodies and muscles move in time and in unison as one man. The tempo and speed is regulated by the chanting of Negro bondage songs, led by a toil-hardened Negro of years of servitude as follows:

"A long steel rail," croons the leader.

"Ump!" grunt all the rest in chorus as pickaxes come down.

"An' a short cross tie," croons the leader

"Ump!" grunt all the rest in chorus as pickaxes come up.

"It rings lik' sil-vah," croons the leader.

"Ump!" goes the chorus as the picks come down.

"It shin's lik' go-old," croons the leader.

"Ump!" and all the picks come up.

And so it goes all day long, with the torrid rays of the blazing monarch of the skies adding their touch of additional misery.

This working in unison is called "Keeping the lick."

By sundown every prisoner is completely exhausted from the long hours of back-breaking toil in the terrific heat of a semi-tropical sun. Covered with a slime created of the mixture of human sweat and the dust of the dirt roads, we go back to camp, weary and fatigued of body; expressionless of soul and mind as men in a drug-induced coma.

Still unwashed, in our chains and stinking rags we sit down to a cold supper of corn pone, middlings and sorghum—supper is identical, too, for every night in the year.

Supper over, we are locked in the bull pen, and lights are promptly put out at 8:30 P.M.

Locked in the bull pen after my first day's toil, I found most of the other thirty-two convicts grouped around me all asking questions at once. Who was I? where did I come from? How long did I have?

"Say, are you Burns, that editor guy from Chicago?" queried M. B. Hooper, doing four years for a heist in Savannah. Hooper was the hero of the Floyd Collins episode at Crystal Cave, Kentucky.

"Yes," I answered.

"Well, you got a tough break, and you're in a tough joint, get that, brother," replied Hooper. "I escaped once but they caught me the same day and here I am—but if I get a chance I'm going to go again."

"So you're Burns, eh? Looks to me like you're good for seven years here, and boy this *is* one mean stir. Hang it on the limb if you get a chance—I'm going at the first break."

The speaker was Jack Kaufman, safecracker, holdup artist and all around bad man. He had escaped from La Grange five years before, pulled a job in South Carolina, was caught and sent up for four years. After finishing that stretch he had been sent back to La Grange to complete the five to fifteen bit he owed to Georgia.

"How's State and Madison Streets, Kid? Still there, I hope," spoke up hard-boiled Jack Martin, killer, heist guy, pete man and jail breaker extraordinary. Originally sentenced to ten years in Florida, he escaped. While a fugitive from Florida he killed a rich broker in Macon, Georgia, who didn't reach for a cloud fast enough, and fled to Tennessee. Brought back, tried and sentenced to life on the Georgia chain gangs, he escaped again. Freedom, however, only meant another caper for Jack Martin, and he received life in Michigan when a copper was bumped off during a pete job in Detroit. While serving his time on that rap in Jackson prison, Michigan, the Georgia authorities located him, and he was pardoned by the Governor of Michigan so he could finish his life in the Georgia chain gangs.

He escaped the third time but was captured in Atlanta eight months later. Three loaded automatics were found on him when he was caught the last time. And now—here he was at La Grange.

"You can't edit any magazines here, Mr. Al Capone, from Chicago."

This wise crack came from Dick Galloway, Atlanta's millionaire college boy thrill slayer, who with Harsh, another college boy, got life for killing an Atlanta druggist in a thrill stick-up. When Dick Galloway first went to prison he enjoyed a soft job at "The Farm," in Milledgeville; but he was finally sent to La Grange in chains for helping a fellow prisoner at "The Farm" in an attempted escape.

"So you're back in the gang again, eh! Gone seven years, but home again. Well, I beat them, too—they brought me back from Texas—but I am going again. I'm gon'a hand it right back to them, and if you're smart you'll do the same. Seven years is too damn long."

This advice came from "Bounce" Murphy—a local boy—sentenced to twelve months for a pint of moonshine. He escaped only to be recaptured in Texas and brought back with an additional twelve months added to his time.

"So you're Burns, eh? Well I'll be damned—if you ain't pretty, being away fur seven years and then land back here. I cain't read—but I've heard tolerable about ye. Let me get away, I'll *never* come back."

Those remarks came from Ellis Ingram, typical native Georgia cracker, two-time loser, serving his second rap—twelve months for auto stealing.

"Lights out in three minutes! Quiet, up there!"

The booming voice of Doc Adamson, trusty, serving twenty years for rape—and at the moment acting as night watchman.

At this signal, all of us lay on our bunks. Sleeping accommodations consisted of an iron cot, a dirty straw mattress, still dirtier cotton pillow and a blanket so glazed with dirt as to feel slimy to the touch.

In a minute the lights went out and the bull pen was in darkness. I lay on my cot and reflected on my predicament.

Here I was, in the toughest chain gang in Georgia, thrown in with the most desperate of Georgia's felons. Every state convict at the La Grange stockade was there because he was considered a tough egg, and almost to a man, every one was planning to "hang it on the limb" if vigilance wavered or the opportunity beckoned.

Discipline was strict—and with each attempted break it would get stricter. Environment makes the man. I felt I would rather be dead than in such a place for seven years.

With so many convicts planning and plotting for a chance to escape, who would be the first to try? Who would actually make it?

Escape! It was the dream and the hope of every convict who lay sweating there on that torrid July night in what represented a prison in Georgia.

This in Twentieth Century America, the land of ideals, human justice, liberty and progress.

CHAPTER XVI

Excitement Among the Convicts

WITH SUCH an assortment of men, hardened and made desperate by the inhuman treatment that faced them day by day, excitement was always just around the corner.

One day "Bounce" Murphy feigned sickness. He was kept locked in the bull pen. About 9 o'clock "Old Rakestraw," the yard boss, passed him a cup of coffee and a dose of salts through the bars. When the rest of the chain gang had completed their labors, and were back in the stockade eating supper, the bull-pen door would be unlocked and the sick, if they were able, would come down to get their ration of corn pone and middlings. If unable to get up, there they lay until around 8 P.M., when Doc Adamson, trusty night watchman, might enter the bull pen and look them over. Adamson was only a trusty and by no means a physician, yet his word was final. The man was sick or well.

"Bounce" had somehow managed to secure a hack-saw blade and smuggle it into the bull pen. Knowing the routine of the stockade, he conceived a bold and desperate plan. After the main body of convicts and guards left the camp for the roads, "Old Rakestraw" was the only guard on duty in the stockade.

With one eye peeled for the old man, "Bounce" got out his hack saw and went to work. To cover up the sound of the blade as it slowly bit into the hard steel bars, he alternately sang and cursed in loud harsh tones. That day he nearly severed two bars. He filled the cracks with dirt. On the following day he intended to play off sick again, complete the sawing of the bars, overpower "Old Rake-straw," take his keys and gun and make a bid for freedom.

His plan was perfect and almost complete, but that night he made a fatal mistake. He took some of the other convicts into his confidence and offered them an opportunity to go with him. Before "lights out" that night half of the prisoners knew about the planned break; and two, Jack Kaufman and a con named Powell, planned to go with him the next day.

Excitement was in the air when Adamson's "Everybody up and I mean you!" rang out at 3 A.M. Bounce, Powell and Kaufman did not file out—they lay in their bunks, sick.

There are always "stools" in every prison. Someone passed the word to a guard, the guard passed it on higher up.

Action was swift and punishment sure. A score of guards dragged the three out of the bull pen and placed them in the "jack."

"So you don't like my chain gang," roared Warden Hardy. "Well, I'll try and make it nice and comfortable for you all. Perhaps you all will like it better when I get through with you—take off your shoes!"

The "jack" is a relic of the ancient Spanish Inquisition—a medieval instrument of human torture. The three convicts sat on a bench in front of the "jack." Each held his arms and legs straight out at right angles to his body. At the command of the warden they placed both hands and feet through holes specially arranged to receive them. With their hands and feet correctly in place the Warden worked a long lever which locked the convicts' hands and feet in the holes by means of the boards coming together on their ankles and wrists, and holding them securely.

The lever was now locked in place and the bench on which the convicts were sitting was pulled from under them. This left the three convicts hanging in midair by their ankles and wrists, while their hands and feet protruded on the other side. Held in this fashion the convicts were unable to move a muscle, and soon their bodies became taut and strained to the point of excruciating torture.

There they hung in agony for one solid hour.

When the lever was unlocked they fell to the floor completely paralyzed. It was almost one half hour before they could walk without assistance. This was only the beginning of their tortures. These three were to be an example.

After passing his hour in the "jack," Bounce was thrown into the sweat box. The sweat box is three feet square and six feet high. There is one small door, and when Bounce was locked inside, he could neither lie down nor sit down, and was in total darkness. The box was exposed to the rays of the fierce tropical sun. Ventilation was limited to a few small holes bored near the top.

Once each twenty-four hours a cup of water and a chunk of corn pone was passed inside. Bounce was kept locked in the sweat box for three nights and two days! On the third day, he was removed from the box.

As there was only one box Powell and Kaufman received a different treatment.

"Pickshacks" were locked on their left legs and they were detailed to the heaviest work. A "pickshack" is a bar of steel about thirty inches long. It weighs ten pounds. It is hinged in the center and an iron band allows it to be locked on and around the calf of the leg, by means of a Yale padlock. This is worn in addition to the shackles and chains.

Neither Powell nor Kaufman could walk without dragging the left foot with a peculiar limp. The weight of the pickshack put a constant unnatural strain on the muscles of their legs—but nevertheless they had to "keep the lick."

Think of fifteen and a half hours a day of endless toil, in the heat of a Georgia sun, feet chained together and a pickshack locked on your leg. That *is* torture!

That night, an official entered the bull pen with two iron necklaces. A necklace is a heavy iron collar and five feet of heavy chain.

"Where do you sleep?" he asked of Kaufman.

"Here," replied Kaufman indicating his cot.

"Sit on your bunk."

Kaufman complied.

The official then placed the iron collar around Kaufman's neck and locked it in place with a huge padlock. Next he fixed the other end of the chain to an iron ring that was imbedded in the concrete floor.

Kaufman was now chained to the floor with five feet of heavy chain secured at his throat by means of the iron collar and the padlock. The chain was just long enough to allow him to lie down on his cot.

Powell received the identical fate.

Their pickshacks were unlocked and placed under their cots, ready to be relocked on in the morning.

Chains on feet, chained to the floor, pickshacks and padlocks! No wonder they call it a chain gang.

When Bounce came out of the box he also received a "pickshack," and a "La Grange necklace." For ninety days Bounce, Powell and Kaufman wore their steel decorations.

The harder the discipline, the harder the convict becomes. Cruelty brings only one result. Revolt! Constant fear makes the weak strong and the strong stronger.

Dick Galloway had brains, money, friends. He also had life. He wore shackles and chains. The first step to escape is to be able to shed the chains at will. Even though the shackles and chains were closely examined twice each day, many schemes were invented to shed the chains; schemes that defied detection. Dick Galloway figured out a scheme.

He smuggled two files and a half dozen small stove bolts into the bull pen and secreted them in his mattress.

The shackles were fastened on the convicts by a small rivet. This rivet was *pronged* into the shape of a little round ball cut in half.

Dick's scheme was to file off the rivet, put a stove bolt in its place, screw the nut up tight, and then file both the nut and the head of the bolt to resemble the rivet. He would have to start and complete the job in one night, as the shackles and chains were examined both on entering and leaving the bull pen.

He waited until Saturday night, as the convicts were not released from the bull pen until after 9 A.M. Sundays. To secure secrecy he did not begin until after 11 P.M., when most of the convicts were asleep. By 6 o'clock Sunday morning he was finished. Instead of rivets in his shackles, he now had bolts with a nut resembling a rivet which he could unscrew at will. The first step toward liberty was taken.

All the following week while at work on the roads he waited for a chance to make the break for freedom. But when the test came he either lost his nerve or else did not think the time opportune.

Bounce, Powell and Kaufman all worked in Dick's gang. The next Saturday night he took them into his confidence, and one by one all three doctored their shackles in a similar manner.

When the time was right all four were going to go at once!

Fate intervened and changed the plan. Dick got back his soft job on "The Farm."

Bounce, Powell and Kaufman were left to go it alone. None of the three had the intelligence of Galloway. They agreed to play lone hands.

Warden Hardy heard rumors of a plot. On general principles he put the works to Bounce, as Bounce had openly sworn he would escape or die.

Placed on the jack five times in one day, Bounce stuck to his guns. Through a terrific beating he never squawked.

A special guard was appointed over Bounce. The guard had nothing to do but watch him.

The following Saturday morning great excitement prevailed. The whole camp was in an uproar. Bounce had escaped. He had caught his special guard napping for an instant, and in that instant like a flash Bounce was in the underbrush, and like a phantom gone!

All work was stopped. The bloodhounds were brought out, all the guards mobilized for a general hunt. Night came and went and still no trace of Bounce.

That evening, with all the convicts and guards assembled in the mess hall, Warden Hardy fired the special guard. Speaking to the guards but really for the convicts' ears he said, "Don't try to catch the next one who goes—kill him on the spot. Shoot him down! There'll be no more escapes here while I am Warden."

Sunday morning, while attempting to sneak home for clothes and money, Bounce was captured by two members of a citizen posse of La Grange. They received the fifty dollar reward.

Bounce was punished and transferred to the Floyd county gang near Rome, Georgia. Here he tried another get away—and failed.

Altogether Bounce took plenty of punishment.

All for a pint of moonshine!

The convicts go to and from their work in Ford trucks. The drivers are trusties. Several trusties completed their time, and Ellis Ingram was one selected to fill a vacancy. He drove an old model-T, that could not make over twenty miles an hour.

One day he was sent back to the camp alone for some tools. He never reached the stockade. Two days later the truck was found at Gainesville, Georgia, several hundred miles away.

The truck was painted in such a manner, besides carrying special license plates, that it obviously was prison property. A general alarm was sounded and police and sheriffs notified all over the State, but Ellis Ingram got through the highways, several large towns and the city of Atlanta, in that truck.

Three months later he was discovered walking along a highway four miles from the La Grange stockade. Deputy Warden Mobley happened to be passing in his car and captured him.

The next day in chains, stripes and a pickshack Ellis Ingram was doing his fifteen and a half a day for his native State. The county judge added eight months to his time, so that he wouldn't forget that the law is supreme.

In the meantime Powell and Kaufman were still wearing their doctored shackles. Each was waiting for the other to make the break first.

Powell finally got tired of waiting. Thinking he would curry favor, he had a private talk with the warden and confessed the plot.

The warden had every cot torn apart in a search for the files. They were found.

Every single convict was punished; Powell and Kaufman received new shackles and chains, five trips to the jack, a pickshack and necklace for ninety days.

The next night, Kaufman beat Powell's face to a jelly, breaking his nose and dislocating his jaw. Powell was branded as a squealer and his life was made miserable by all the rest of the gang.

"Cowboy" was a Negro lad. Tall, slim, lithe, good-looking and about eighteen years old. Cowboy's nickname came from the fact that he was convicted of stealing three cows. He got three to five years for each cow; nine to fifteen years in all! He had been in the county jail six months, and arrived at the La Grange stockade on a torrid day in August.

After six months in jail it's pretty tough for the first few weeks in the chain gang. Muscles, heart and lungs must get used to the strain of bitter toil. Feet, legs and body must get used to the heavy shackles and chains. The first few days are agony, and "keeping the lick" is impossible.

His first day out Cowboy couldn't "keep the lick." He begged and pleaded for a rest. It was 11 in the morning, the sun was a demon in the sky, burning and scorching everything it touched. It burned Cowboy's skin, tender from imprisonment in jail, it seared his soul and befuddled his brain. Cowboy was out, but still on his feet, and in a pitiful plea he futilely begged the guard for a rest.

In a tender and soothing voice the guard answered his agonized plea.

"Lay your shovel down, Cowboy, and come here."

Cowboy obeyed.

Standing face to face with the guard, the guard continued in his most pleasant voice.

"What's the matter, Cowboy, can't you make it."

"No, sir, boss—I'll have to toughen up a bit."

"Yes, I reckon you will," and with that the guard hauled off and socked the dumbfounded Cowboy square on the jaw.

The blow was terrific and so unexpected it felled poor Cowboy like a log. And while the half-insensible boy lay prone at his feet, the guard deliberately kicked him in the face and stomach.

"Get up and go to work you *son-of-a-bitch!* I'll learn ye to rest! There's no rest for Niggers in this chain gang!"

Half fainting and in despair blacker than his skin, the helpless Cowboy dragged his body to his shovel and in mortal terror attempted to go on with his toil. The dinner hour saved him from complete collapse.

During the dinner hour the guard cut a stout hickory limb and taunted Cowboy with it during the noonday rest period. "If you don't keep the lick this afternoon, I'll break this limb on your damn Nigger hide. Do you understand?"

Cowboy understood only too well.

That afternoon Cowboy was beaten unconscious with that hickory limb.

"Nub" had forty years. He had been in the chain gang now going on six years. During his first winter in the gang all his toes were frozen and were amputated. Hence his nickname "Nub." Nub was colored. For six years he wore the same set of chains. From the first day and every other day for the six years those chains had never been off of poor Nub. Not even when the county doctor cut off his toes.

Nub's forebears had been slaves. Nub's life was doomed to worse than slavery. Forty years in the chain gang is quite a load. Twice he tried to escape and failed. It was certain he would try again. There was nothing else to do.

"Indiana" was Nub's pal and sidekick. They worked and slept side by side. Negroes can be real pals. Friendship in misery is a special characteristic of Negroes.

Indiana had ten years. He got away once, but was caught in the state of Indiana, hence his nickname. Neither one could read or write, nevertheless they exhibited a flash of real brains in the trick they pulled in making an escape, even though a special guard was appointed just to watch them. The guard carried a shotgun and a revolver.

Soil was being hauled from near-by farms to the road in Model-A Ford automatic dump trucks. A lever similar and next to the emergency brake controlled the dumping apparatus. When this lever was pushed forward the front part of the body rose high in the air, and the soil slid out the rear end. When the truck was empty the body was lowered by pulling this lever back.

Nub and Indiana and their special guard were on the road, the balance of the gang and the rest of the guards were in the soil pit about a quarter of a mile away. By operating ten trucks, a load of soil was dumped on the road every five minutes. The routine was as follows:

"Dump the next one here," the guard would say, indicating a low place in the road. Nub and Indiana would then stand on either side of the low place. The driver of the approaching truck would know from experience that he was to drive the truck between them. When the truck was in the right spot, Nub and Indiana would cry out "Hold it!" and the driver would stop and dump the truck by pushing the lever. The body would rise in the air, the soil slide out, and the truck would restart, the empty body still in the air.

The driver never left his seat, the engine never stopped running. The truck would pull away and the driver would lower the body on the way back to the pit. The truck drivers were trusties.

A speed governor was attached to each truck to limit the speed to twenty-five miles an hour.

Grady, a twenty-one-year-old boy, serving five years, had been made a trusty and this was his second day on a truck. He pulled in between Nub and Indiana, heard them cry "Hold it!" and dumped his truck. The guard at the time was standing about twelve feet back of the truck. As Grady dumped the truck, Indiana came forward and said, "Grady, the rear spring is broke, you'd better look at it and tell Boss Hancock to get it fixed."

Grady got out of the driver's seat to look at the rear end. When he reached the back of the truck it started to move away.

Grady and the guard stood in speechless amazement.

As Grady stepped out of the driver's seat, Indiana had stepped in from one side and Nub stepped in from the other. Indiana shifted the gears silently and away they went up the road. It was useless for the guard to shoot as both were protected from bullets by the steel body high in the air, which afforded them complete protection.

The guard fired his gun to warn the other guards and cried out, "Nub and Indiana's gone!"

Bedlam followed. The next approaching truck was dumped before it reached the road, the governor pulled off, two guards jumped in and the race started, as Nub and Indiana were still in sight.

Indiana was not dumb. Up the road a bit he stopped the truck, pulled off the governor also, jumped back in and opened her up for all she was worth. *Then* he lowered the body.

At fifty-five miles an hour on a winding country pike Nub and Indiana were soon out of sight. The two guards in the second truck kept right on, as they were sure the runaways would ditch the truck somewhere along the road and take to the woods.

The governor was pulled off a third truck and it started at top speed for the stockade eighteen miles away, to set the alarm and get the bloodhounds. All work was stopped and the rest of the convicts herded into a small group while the balance of the guards, with shotguns ready for instant action, stood over them.

On the way to the stockade the third truck was wrecked, which delayed the hunt an hour or more.

Nub and Indiana stopped the truck at a dense woods, jumped out, bade each other good-by and dived into the woods from opposite sides of the road. Better that one should be caught than both.

Nub ran to a near-by farm house, found an axe and cut off his chains. Looking further he discovered an old pair of overalls, discarded his stripes, donned the overalls and again made for the cover of the woods. Like a hunted animal guided by instinct instead of reason, he headed directly for the swamps in which Georgia abounds.

Indiana on his side of the woods also located a farm house, found the always ready axe at the wood pile and cut off his chains. Unable to find any clothes, he took off his stripes anyway and dived into the woods nude.

Two illiterate Negroes, battling for freedom in the wilds of Georgia's swamps, hunted by white men like beasts of prey. For more than two hundred years the woods and swamps of Georgia have witnessed similar exciting scenes.

And even before that in the wilds of Africa the tragedy was enacted, the purpose the same, the result foretold.

In less than two hours the warden, guards, eight bloodhounds and a small posse reached the abandoned truck. The dogs were let loose and the hunt was on. Bloodhounds may lose the trail of a white man, but never a Negro. A Negro leaves something in his footprints that a bloodhound enjoys.

And what is it in a Negro's make-up that strikes him with mortal terror when he hears the bay of the hounds? And, when he sees the hounds, to make for a tree?

Nub was caught first. They found him perched in a tree like a monkey, his eyes wild with fright, the dogs barking, jumping and circling the tree.

An hour later, as naked as the day he was born, Indiana was found gibbering in another tree, and dogs cutting up high jinks at his feet.

What a laugh the guards and the posse get out of this fear of Negroes for bloodhounds. It's hard to say who enjoys it the most, the dogs or the white men.

Nub and Indiana were given a scientific punishment, a half dozen trips to the jack, the heaviest chains procurable and were back on the job next day.

Nub will die in chains unless he escapes. In five or six years Indiana's time will be up.

With all these failures before him, and the punishments that follow, who would have the courage to try to beat the impossible? But the battle of wits never ceases. The captive is always trying to escape. Since man invented prisons and slavery, the prisoners and the slaves have always attempted to escape, regardless of the price of failure. The battle has gone on for thousands of years. It will go on for thousands of years to come.

It is almost a year since Cowboy came to the chain gang. He is still in stripes and chains, but he has not forgotten the punishment he received on his first day, nor that he got since then.

Cowboy has hardened to his plight. He is nineteen now. During a year in the chain gang, he has learned many things he did not know before. One is that human sympathy is only in the dictionary. Another is that this is a world where the fit win and the unfit fail.

Victory embraces the shrewd, the daring, the cunning and fearless. Failure hugs the docile, the weaklings and the coward. Cowboy could not express these thoughts in words, but he could translate them into action.

He is in a different crew now, under a different guard. He is in Boss Chris's gang.

Boss Chris is in charge of a road scraper crew. The equipment consists of a tractor, a road scraper and an old model-T flat-bodied Ford truck. The Ford is so old and dilapidated it cannot make over twenty miles an hour. Besides himself his crew is made up of: John Arnold, white, lifer and trusty; Squint, a one-eyed Negro, lifer and trusty, and Cowboy.

Their job is to scrape the roads. The four leave the stockade each morning in the Ford, John Arnold driving, Cowboy and Squint sitting on the side, and Boss Chris on the driver's seat next to John Arnold.

At sundown, they pull the tractor and scraper to one side of the road, leave them there and return to camp in the Ford.

The next morning they drive to where they left their tractor and scraper, oil and grease both machines, park the Ford and begin their work. Boss Chris carries a loaded revolver in a holster strapped around his waist. Boss Chris is a tried and trusted guard. Arnold and Squint, the two trusties, through years of servitude, have come to consider the chain gang as their life and their home. Cowboy in stripes and chains is watched and distrusted by all three. That's the layout that confronted Cowboy, and he figured out a perfect escape.

It was a Monday morning in August, 1930, when these four left the La Grange stockade to work on a road near the Alabama line.

They reached the tractor and scraper around 4 A.M. just as the sun was creeping up on the horizon.

"Cowboy, grease that tractor well this morning. It rained Sunday night!" said Boss Chris.

"Yes, sir, Boss," answered Cowboy, as, with grease bucket and paddle in hand, he bent down beside the tractor.

Cowboy worked silently for several minutes, then he cried out, "Look, Boss Chris, someone has been fooling wid dis here tractor."

Boss Chris bent down beside Cowboy to look. For an instant they are side by side, bodies bent peering into the track mechanism of the tractor.

For a long time Cowboy had studied, planned and waited for that instant. With the swiftness and skill of a striking cobra, Cowboy extracted the gun from Boss Chris' holster.

Pointing the gun at Boss Chris he said, "I've waited a long time to get dis, and now I done got it. Step over by the road there."

Arnold and Squint were greasing the scraper further down the road. Cowboy called them, "Oh, John! Oh, Squint!" They came on the run.

When they reached Cowboy's side of the tractor they stood in speechless terror. Turning the gun on them Cowboy ordered them to line up alongside of Boss Chris. Still keeping them covered with the gun, he said, "Somebody is liable to get killed here right sudden if any of you-all try any tricks. I got dis here gun and I'se gwine to get away or somebody gwine to die. I'm boss now! John Arnold, put that hammer and cold chisel on the truck and crank her up."

John Arnold did as he was told, but he was so terror stricken that he did not have the strength left to crank the truck.

"Get away from there," commanded Cowboy, "an' get back in line." Then addressing Squint he continued, "Squint, go and crank that truck and if you don't get it started you die. Get that!"

Squint got it all right, and in cringing fear, had the engine running in a moment. It beat a song of life and liberty for Cowboy.

Still holding the gun Cowboy jumped on the truck, threw in the clutch, and started up the road toward the Alabama line.

The last view of Cowboy faded out of sight as he sat at the wheel, still holding the gun in two fingers of one hand, while steering the car.

Two hours later one of the greatest manhunts in that region was under way. Cars of every description and a posse of one hundred were searching for Cowboy, but no Cowboy was ever found.

The next day the truck was found one hundred and twenty miles away, in the State of Alabama. Warden Hardy's records show the following entry: "_____ (Cowboy's name) age nineteen, gingerbread color, five feet, eight inches, weight about 140 lbs., serving nine to fifteen years, for cow stealing, escaped August 20, 1930."

Cowboy came to the chain gang a quiet, simple, easygoing, harmless darkey. He escaped, with a revolver in his possession, a fearless, dangerous and desperate criminal.

Somewhere in the United States today is Cowboy, with a scar on his heart and a brand on his brain. To him "the law" is not something to respect—it is something he hates; he will kill, before he will let it again place its chains of bondage on his body.

CHAPTER XVII

A Hearing before the Prison Commission

W ITH EVERYONE around me plotting to escape I determined to put my faith in the Prison Commission's sense of justice. I felt I merited a parole or a pardon.

Worried and in despair, I still clung to the faint hope that the Prison Commission would never dare to turn my clemency petition down since I had repaid the State all its expense and I knew the character testimony taken in Judge David's court had already reached Attorney Howard by mail. And at this very moment hundreds of letters and telegrams from all over the country were pouring in to both the Governor and the Prison Commission, requesting my release on the basis of Christianity and American fair play and justice.

The Prison Commission, when questioned by reporters and those interested in my case for the reason for my transfer to Troup County, gave out the following statement:

"We sent Burns to Troup County for safekeeping, as this woman from Chicago visited him alone at the other camp and brought liquor to him there."

This charge I emphatically brand as a deliberate untruth, since at no time did Lillian Salo visit me except when accompanied by one of my Atlanta attorneys, and at no time did she bring me a single drop of liquor. This refutation can be positively verified by the Warden, guards and prisoners at Campbell County.

Here again was the invisible hand of subtle innuendo still following me right down into the chain gang. That invisible hand!

The first hearing for my clemency petition was held on August 10, 1929, at the offices of the Prison Commission in Atlanta, Georgia. On this day, while my fate hung in the balance, I was laboring like a Trojan beneath the cruel, broiling rays of a fierce midsummer sun. Garbed in the stripes of a desperate felon, I was engaged in the backbreaking toil of loading trucks with soil, keeping time with a gang of Negroes at the rate of sixteen shovelfuls a minute, thirteen hours a day.

Not being at the hearing, my record here of what went on was obtained by me through my brother, who did attend the hearing, and by way of the reports of it published in the Georgia newspapers. Quite a number of persons attended and the hearing was called to order by Chairman Rainey with the following announcement:

"We will now hear the Burns Case, and will limit the hearing to thirty minutes."

Thirty minutes! It would have been utterly impossible to even casually glance over the immense number of letters and affidavits and the court records from Chicago in an hour!

Attorney John F. Echols came first. He related to the Commission briefly the circumstances of my original arrest and conviction. He cited my war record and declared that starvation had faced me when I succumbed to the temptation of robbery.

My brother, the Reverend Vincent Burns, was next. He made an impassioned appeal for mercy for me, reviewing my life's history and making the declaration that this one misdeed was my only crime. He called upon the Commission in the name of Christianity and American justice to return me to the life that I had rehabilitated for myself in Chicago.

He was followed by Doctor C. O. Jones, head of the Georgia Anti-Saloon League, who made a brief plea for both clemency and mercy, quoting scriptural references which he said were pertinent to the case. Doctor Jones was then followed by representatives of the Elks, the American Legion and the Federation of Churches, who also made a dramatic plea for my parole.

Then Attorney William Schley Howard summed up the case for me, presenting a stack of letters and affidavits from Chicago business and professional men endorsing my character. He referred to the dictum of Blackstone that "punishment is for reformation and protection of society."

Mr. Howard further claimed that I had proved my reformation and deserved to be freed from prison so that I could take up my life before it was interrupted too long for reclamation.

But—the character testimony taken under oath in John David s court at Chicago the day before I left there *was not presented to the Prison Commission.*

Assistant Solicitor Edward A. Stephens then appeared for the State. He said that I had fought extradition when arrested in May and had sought to evade justice. He denied that I had reformed and had become an exemplary citizen. He introduced an affidavit, sworn to by my wife, in which he charged that I had previously married in Chicago, under the alias of Edward J. O'Brien, a woman named Jean McDonald, and had never been divorced. Thus, he claimed, my marriage to Emily had been bigamous. This affidavit contained many additional grave charges, and he further declared that I was now liable for criminal prosecution if the State of Illinois cared to press the case.

In addition, he declared, I had started my business by borrowing $2,500 from my wife, which I had never repaid, and that I had left her in misery and want while I lived in ease and luxury.

Mr. Stephens also submitted a copy of the Chicago *Evening American* of May 24, 1928, in which appeared a story under my signature reciting the harrowing cruelties of Georgia prison life. He concluded his remarks by saying that I was a menace to society and was entitled to neither mercy nor clemency.

Mr. Howard, in a brief rebuttal, denied all the allegations and introduced as evidence a stack of checks made out by me to my wife or endorsed and cashed by her that totalled nearly $8,000. This closed the hearing and the Commissioners took the case under advisement.

CHAPTER XVIII

Some Interesting Sidelights on Chain-Gang Life

WHILE THE judicial minds of the Prison Commission were pondering the weighty problem of my fate, based on their principles of humanity and justice, I was daily facing the ordeal of a living hell.

To properly describe the mental and physical torture of a Georgia chain gang baffles and beggars my powers of description. Upon arriving at the Troup County stockade, I found conditions that were almost identical with those in Fulton and Campbell Counties seven years ago. There was but one difference—they were worse!

In place of the lash, which I have already explained had been abolished in 1923 by an executive order of Governor Walker, an ancient barbaric and mediaeval instrument of torture had been introduced. *This was the stocks invented in the days of the Spanish Inquisition.*

Almost every night when we would return to the stockade after thirteen hours of heart-breaking toil, three or four of the convicts would be introduced to the "jack" (as the stocks were called), for no other reason than that they did not work hard enough to suit the whim of some illiterate and ignorant guard.

Although I mentioned the "jack" in a previous chapter, I think another word here will not be amiss. The "jack" looks exactly like the pictures you have seen of the stocks used in this country during Puritan times in Massachusetts. The terror-stricken victim sits on a bench, placing his hands and feet between boards that have notches cut out to receive them. When he is in the proper position, the Warden pulls a lever which forces the boards together, brutally squeezing convict's wrists and ankles.

After the lever is locked in place, the bench on which the convict sits is pulled from under him and he finds himself suspended in mid-air, hanging by his wrists and ankles.

He is kept in this state of excruciating torture for one hour. Think of it! While the convict is thus suffering the agonies of Hell, the Warden and the guards take comfortable, reposing positions and punctuate his shrieks of pain with laughter and such expressions as "I don't feel no pain" and "How can you feel any—I am resting comfortably?"

The State Law of Georgia specifically states that no prisoner, black or white, can be placed in the stocks without first being examined by the County Physician, who must be present while the prisoner is in it.

In the thirteen months that I was at Troup County stockade, this rule was enforced but once, in the face of an average of six punishments weekly such as I have described.

There were many other violations of the state laws, which were as follows:

The state law of Georgia requires that the rules and regulations governing the conduct and conditions of the convicts by the County Warden be conspicuously placed where all may read them.

The state furnishes large placards bearing these rules in letters a quarter of an inch high. At no time during my stay there were these rules and regulations ever posted in Troup County.

One of these rules, most important to the health and conduct of the convicts, covered bathing facilities. This rule stated that the convicts must get one bath and clean clothes every week of the year and two baths a week during the period from May 1, to October 1. This additional bath, granted by the State, was made necessary by the intense heat of this period.

At no time during my entire stay at Troup County did the convicts ever receive more than one bath each week.

The bathing facilities provided there were of the most primitive and limited nature. We bathed on Saturday afternoons in a combination sleeping quarters and mess hall. Five of the full trusties slept in this room. There were always a total of from eighty to one hundred convicts at this camp.

Although the stockade was a cement building, it was devoid of all plumbing and simple sanitation. Bath tubs were improvised by sawing in half large casks. There were never more than twenty of these make-shift bath tubs in use at one time.

On Saturday afternoons they would be stacked outside of the convicts' entrance to the stockade, and the first twenty convicts in the building would each grab a tub, making it necessary for the remainder to wait until these twenty had bathed and emptied their tubs.

The first twenty convicts who were fortunate in securing a tub would carry them into the building and place them around the mess hall, in between the tables.

Our Saturday dinner, consisting of cow peas and corn-bread, would already be set on these tables in tin plates. While some of the convicts were eating, others were bathing. Those eating would sometimes have to move their tin dish of food to avoid the splash of the bathers.

Water from the nearby creek was placed in tin drums and heated over an open fire. It was carried from there by buckets into the building. Because of this scarcity and difficulty in procuring water, only one bucket was allowed each convict—an amount barely sufficient to wash his feet.

So that you may have some conception of how dirty and filthy the convicts were by Saturday at bathing-time, picture a man being ducked in water, clothes and all, then rolled in the dust while still wet, twice a day for six consecutive days, during which time he had not even washed his hands or changed his clothes, and there you have our condition on Saturday afternoons.

The heat of the Georgia sun was so great that every day our clothes and bodies became wringing wet with perspiration and the dust from the dirt roads upon which we worked would settle on our bodies like frosting on a cake.

One bucket of water for a man in that condition! This Saturday bath was more of a gesture than anything else.

Towels, handkerchiefs or other personal articles were extremely scarce, the majority of the convicts having no personal possessions of any description. But if you were the exception, you would have to wash your towels and personal clothing in the same water and tub that you had used to bathe in.

The chains that the convicts wore were riveted to their ankles and were as much a part of their physical being as their arms or legs. These chains would drag on the ground and become caked with filth. When the convict stepped into the tub, the chain and its collection of grime went along with him.

In this way were the two baths a week prescribed by the State enforced at Troup County.

The regulations specifically required that all bedding be sunned at least once a week and that linen and blankets, etc., be washed once a week. Perhaps at some of the other camps this rule may have been observed, but at Troup County during my stay, we enjoyed the luxury of clean bedding but twice.

The sleeping quarters consisted of a large, bare room, enclosed on three sides by solid cement walls and on the fourth by iron bars, which looked into the main corridor of the building. The ceiling and floor also were of solid cement. This was known as the bull pen.

Moveable iron cots were arranged in two rows along the walls in the bull pen. Our bedding consisted of a cheap straw mattress, one pillow and a blanket, all of which were heavily glazed with dirt, and reeking with pungent odors. It was hard to tell which was the filthiest—our sweaty, mud-caked clothes and bodies, or our nauseating bedding.

Looking in through the corridor bars you would observe the following sight in the bull pen. A double row of iron cots. On each cot, a convict in a different stage of dress or undress. There is one stark naked with his clothes lying on the floor beside his cot. Here is another lying on his cot completely dressed, too exhausted even to remove his clothes. Another has merely removed his shirt, unequal to the Houdini-like trick of passing his trousers through the iron shackles on his ankles.

Down the center of the bull pen is a row of large iron rings securely embedded in the concrete. You would notice a heavy iron chain running from one of these iron rings in the floor to a second iron ring around the convict's neck, and held in position by a huge Yale padlock at his throat. Two of the resting convicts are thus secured. This was additional torture to the aforementioned "jack" and part of the fine art of punishment of a Georgia chain gang.

You would also see a large galvanized tub on a soap box near the bars. This contained our drinking water. On the box, beside the tub, was a dipper which was used by all. At the rear of the bull pen you would note two iron buckets. These constituted our toilets. We were usually locked up in the bull pen around 7 o'clock in the evening, and were led out at about 3:30 A.M. every morning excepting Sunday when we were permitted to sleep until 8 o'clock.

Leaving the bull pen at this early hour on week-days, we were herded into the mess hall where our breakfast was already on the table. The majority of the prisoners were unable to read and write and were typical "hillbillies," never having been more than fifty miles away from the scene of their birth. Thus they lacked knowledge of the outside world and its common decencies and saw no hardship in not washing their hands or faces or cleaning their teeth before the morning meal. But to those who were the exception and were accustomed to the simple refinements of civilization, a slight provision was made for their morning toilette. This consisted of a tub of water and a filthy basin that leaked profusely in one corner of the mess hall and if one cared to wash he must do without soap, as none was provided or accessible at that time. This one basin was the only facility for thirty white prisoners. Since a limited time was allotted for breakfast, washing was a luxury enjoyed only by the first few reaching the basin.

Breakfast over, we would pass out in single file into the yard and stand in three groups in the early morning darkness.

The first group, under Boss Hancock, was known as the soil-pit gang. The work in this gang was the hardest of any and so was the boss.

The second group was known as the wheeler squad and was under the direction of Boss Wright. The work in this squad was nothing like that of the soil-pit and, in truth, there was also a great difference between Boss Wright and Boss Hancock.

The third squad was known as the wagon crew and was under the supervision of Boss Louie Bowles. White prisoners assigned to this group were lucky, for the work was lighter for them than in either of the other two groups. Boss Louie Bowles was the most intelligent and considerate of any of the bosses at the camp.

In each group whites and Negroes worked side by side, which was another violation of the state regulation. All of the groups left the camp in Ford trucks going in different directions to the scene of their respective labors.

While the Prison Commission was considering my first application for parole I was working in the soil-pit group. Our work consisted of loading top soil from nearby farms into trucks which conveyed it to the roads.

On arriving at the soil-pit (that immediate section of the farm where we would obtain the top soil), the nine or ten trucks would form a semi-circle with four shovelers alongside of each truck. The three guards assigned to this group would place themselves in strategic positions facing the trucks on the same side at which the shovelers were located. When this formation had been properly completed, work would commence.

The first prisoner of the first group at the first truck would then set the pace at which we would all shovel. As he went down for the first shovelful, all the other prisoners were supposed to go down with him, and as he came up with the loaded shovel, all the other prisoners were to come up also, and as he threw the dirt into the wagon, all were supposed to follow in rhythm and, as his shovel would click when the edge of it hit the wagon, all of the others were to hit at the same time. That is how we "kept the lick."

Once the shovelling commenced, the guards would watch to see that every prisoner kept pace with the leader, and no excuses or alibis were accepted for failure to keep the pace. At the first crack of dawn the work commenced and continued without any let-up whatsoever until 11:30 A.M. As the first truck was loaded it pulled out to the road, usually only a very short distance away. The second truck then moved up to where the first had been and all other trucks moved up accordingly. The first truck now, having dumped its load on the road, came back into the pit and became the last truck.

Under this arrangement, the convicts were kept everlastingly shovelling from dawn to sunset. The speed of the lick was usually sixteen shovelfuls a minute or 960 shovelfuls an hour.

Is your imagination equal to conceiving what torture this may be . . . continued for thirteen hours a day . . . handicapped by shackles and chains . . . in the blazing heat of a tropical sun . . . six days a week . . . month in and month out . . . year after year?

CHAPTER XIX

The Depths of Despair

AUGUST 24, 1929, at which time I was a member of the soil-pit gang, was an exceptionally hot and dusty day, even for Georgia.

I had been keeping the lick all morning in the terrific heat.

It had been two weeks since the Prison Commission had heard my case and they had not as yet arrived at a decision.

All morning I had wearily kept pace with the sweating Negro beside me. My hands were blistered, my feet were sore and the muscles of my back were tormenting demons. As I worked in silence, my mind, as a thing apart, played tricks with my imagination.

Was this real, or was this only a dream? The thought of my office in Chicago, its mahogany desk and shining glass top . . . the comfortable chair in which I used to sit . . . clean and well clothed and at ease . . . by this time the office force would have been paid off . . . my duties for the week would have been ended . . . and I would have been looking forward with happiness to the arrival of Lillian Salo as she would appear as a beautiful picture in the doorway, fresh, young, beautiful and smiling . . . coming to the office so that we might go out to luncheon . . . ah, good food and ideal surroundings . . . would I ever see it again? . . . How would it taste now . . . And Lillian? Where was she now? . . . Since the Prison Commission had forbidden her to visit me and had ordered her out of Georgia . . . where had all these things gone . . . how had they dissolved into a mist of nothingness and passed out of my life . . . was this still me, garbed in filthy, ragged stripes, sweating and toiling with mechanical rhythm in a foreign land? . . . and while I was thus deeply engrossed in thought, my consciousness was rudely awakened. . . .

"Say, you damned Yankee, go to Work there and get some dirt on that shovel and keep the lick . . ." came the hoarse cry from the guard.

Having been jolted back into my sordid surroundings, I consoled myself with this—the hope that the Prison Commission would parole me soon. With the superabundance of proof submitted to them of my true

109

self, of my upward climb, of my honesty—in short, of my true character, they would let me go. Human beings cannot be so cruel to one another, and I thought of the many editorials that had been written about my case and particularly one in the Ohio State *Journal* of Columbus, Ohio, which read as follows:

"Seven years of lawful activity is more than presumptive evidence of reformation. The theory of legal punishment is the reformation of the prisoner. If he had reformed, what shall it profit Georgia to tear down the reformation? It is inconceivable that chain-gang experience will reform men. How may a man prove his reformation if seven years inside the law brings no consideration? What has Georgia to say to those who tell her she might have tempered her law with human sympathy? She might have given the offender who had straightened out his conduct a fair chance to get ahead in life.

"How will Georgia answer?"

"Well," thought I, as I shoveled, "Georgia will answer soon."

Back in the stockade that afternoon I had not been one of the fortunate twenty to get an early tub and I was sitting on the cook's bed in the mess hall, waiting my turn. The yard boss, "Old" Rakestraw, came over to me and said, "The Commission decided your case. They turned you down."

I just sat and stared at him. Everything seemed to stop. Not even a thought or an emotion of any kind stirred in my numbed body. If ever a person turned to stone, I did at that moment. It is impossible to put down here in words the utter emptiness, emotionless, and mummy-like condition I passed into.

Shortly after this, my mother and brother made another trip to Georgia to appeal to the Governor directly. A few weeks before, on August 17, 1929, the Governor personally wrote to my brother that my case would be considered by him from the highest view of humanity and righteousness.

They believed that the Governor was sincere when he wrote this letter.

With the announcement in the press of the Prison Commission's decision, the Governor and the Prison Commission received hundreds of letters from persons in all walks of life criticizing, or disapproving of, the Commission's decision.

The Governor had the reputation of being a stalwart Christian and a teacher of Sunday School Bible classes, and my mother and brother were unshakeable in their belief that they could move him to compassion.

I would like to remark here that my mother was received in cold contempt by the Christian and hospitable State of Georgia when she called at the office of the Solicitor General with letters of introduction from the Assistant Postmaster General of the United States.

When she called at the office of the Prison Commission, the hostility was not quite so open. Judge Rainey, chairman, explained that reformation played no part in the penitentiary system of Georgia. He said:

"It is not a matter of reformation. Your son owes this state a debt set at six years of labor, and the purpose of the Prison Commission is to collect this debt. If, however, your son makes a good prisoner and a good worker, we may consider his obligation to our State paid in full after he has made one year."

At first the Governor seemed unapproachable, but after great efforts my mother and brother were granted the privilege of an interview.

As they walked into the Governor's office their hearts were filled with hope, for surely, they thought, Georgia's Chief Executive would listen to their plea. The question revolved in their minds . . . *What would the Governor say?*

He listened in stony silence to their pleas and made no comment whatsoever.

Heartbroken, distracted, and nervous, they left for more civilized communities. Alone, and in black despair, I began the weary, ceaseless round of hardship and toil that loomed ahead for at least the next twelve months.

The State law of Georgia specifies that a convict is eligible for parole after twelve months of model conduct, and I determined to meet this requirement.

As though this were not enough trouble to break a man's spirit, the burden was increased by developments taking place in Chicago at about this time.

Some time in September, 1929, my wife filed suit against a leading Chicago newspaper for $100,000, charging slander in articles that appeared in that paper relating to events in our life together during the years of 1924 and 1925. To date, this case has never come to trial.

Her anger still unappeased, she caused the arrest of Merle MacBain, who was now running my paper, for embezzlement. At the preliminary hearing, the judge dismissed the case with the following comment:

"The purpose of the law is not for personal vengeance. It does not and cannot compel a man to live with a woman against his will."

Calling States Attorney Swanson personally to appear before him, the Judge ordered Mr. Swanson to dismiss the case. States Attorney Swanson nolle prossed the charge.

I kept a personal account in the City State Bank of Chicago. In the stock market crash of October, 1929, this bank failed. Now, when I needed funds most, poverty, complete poverty, added to the misery of my lot.

The weary months rolled by and Christmas was approaching. I still had hope that if the true facts of my case were properly presented to Governor Hardmann, he would let me go. In view of this fact, I wrote him a letter at Christmas time and sent it by registered mail through Captain Walsh of the La Grange Branch of the Salvation Army.

I received no acknowledgment of any kind in response to this written personal plea.

CHAPTER XX

Hope Revived Once More

RECREATIONAL AND educational facilities in a Georgia chain gang consist solely of a semi-monthly sermon rendered by an evangelical Baptist minister and the usual background of a few fanatical assistants.

These services took place in the mess hall and all prisoners were compelled to attend them. On one side sat the white prisoners; on the other, the Negro prisoners. Facing both groups, the preacher took his stand, using an old soap box as a pulpit and his assistants sat directly behind him on a wooden bench.

The services almost invariably opened with everyone singing, "The Old-Time Religion" or "The Old Rugged Cross." After the singing of the opening hymn, the minister would deliver a typical, ringing, Baptist sermon profusely sprinkled with "amens" from the group behind him.

He would always finish in the same vein and with the same thought. These were almost his exact words: "If you suffer and are in pain and misery, it is God's will. It matters not what your lot may be, the only thing of earthly importance is to save your soul. If the only way a man's soul might be saved was by hanging him by the neck until dead, or electrocuting him, if these things were the only ways his soul could be saved, it would be better to kill him and save his soul than to let him live and lose his soul."

A great chorus of "amens" would follow his pronouncement and the services would be over.

I don't profess to be a deep student of theology, but somehow I can never accept such a belief. I feel that if a man has a soul he has a responsibility to cultivate it. God or truth can be of help to him. But morally and spiritually a man must learn to stand on his own feet and follow the divine voice that speaks in his own heart.

I had always been a great reader and could really enjoy an interesting book or story, and I began to feel the lack of mental diversion. My mother and Lillian Salo wrote to me regularly every week and their letters were a great consolation to me. Unfortunately, when I escaped the second time I had to leave some of the best of these letters behind.

Some of these letters were glittering jewels of love and loyalty and showed how these two wonderful women suffered with me almost as though they were actually incarcerated with me.

Christmas had come and passed. Relatives, friends and others interested in my plight began to realize that there was grave probability that I might remain on the chain gang for six or seven years more. This fact so appalled them that a great, concentrated and organized movement to obtain my parole at the end of twelve months now got under way.

My mother and brother who were most loyal and untiring in their efforts made numerous trips to Washington and to Chicago. A vain search was made for the particular court stenographer who took down in shorthand the character testimony taken in Judge David's court many months before. It was their hope that in finding him, he might still have the original stenographic notes and so could reproduce this essential document. But he was never located. In place of this my mother, a woman in poor health and along in years, went to Chicago and secured individual and personal sworn affidavits from the same people whose testimony was so mysteriously lost.

Anyone reading these affidavits would see immediately the truth and merit of my cause. There are over eighty of them and they come from some of the highest and most respected individuals in Chicago. Surely so large and influential a group of men and women would not commit perjury to free a menace to society, as I had been labelled by Assistant States Solicitor Stephens.

My brother secured additional affidavits sworn to by responsible persons who knew me before I went overseas to fight for Democracy. To offset any possible trickery or intrigue, photostats of each one of these affidavits were made so that in event of loss it could be immediately replaced.

Winter melted into spring and spring blossomed into summer—still no change was made. My status as a felon destined to daily torture in attempting to repay my debt to the State of Georgia remained the same. The time was approaching when I would soon be eligible for another hearing, which would be in July, 1930.

The bitterest time in a convict's life in Georgia is during the months of June, July, and August, for then the cruel monarch of the heavens bears down with insatiable fury, and by a strange irony of fate, it is at that particular time that the warden and the guards, also feeling the heat, become most cruel and intolerant.

These conditions introduced series of tragedies in the chain gangs of Georgia during the month of June, 1930, when five convicts were literally worked to death. I can only describe the condition surrounding the death of one of them which happened in Troup County. The victim was a Negro whose name I do not recall, but who lived in Hogansville, Georgia, and who had been sentenced the month previous to one year for violation of the State Prohibition Law.

Upon his arrival at the camp, some time in May, he was striped and chained and assigned to work in the soil-pit group. On one exceptionally hot day in June he found it impossible, because of the heat, to keep the lick. He managed, however, to struggle through that day.

On the following morning, he attempted to lay in, claiming that he was sick and unable to work. The Chain Boss "gubered" him (the expression used when a convict claims sickness, but is routed out and put to work by the boss of his group) and put him up in the first group in the soil-pit where he would have to work the hardest.

All morning, as he manfully tried to hold his place, he kept complaining to the guards that he was sick and asked for permission to rest, but without avail. About 3 o'clock he collapsed completely and died within a few minutes. What he actually died from was sunstroke. Intelligent treatment would have saved his life.

His body was roughly thrown in a truck and carried to the camp. That evening a mock coroner's inquest was held in the yard. The Negro's body lay sprawled on the floor of a Ford truck, still clothed in stripes and with the chains of captivity and death on his ankles.

My continuous fight for freedom had now become a matter of state-wide conversation and discussion. Almost all of the better class of Georgians were in favor of my parole. In fact, so many forces were afoot agitating for justice in my case, that it became almost an understood conviction that I would be paroled shortly after my second hearing, which was scheduled for July 9, 1930.

To be sure that everything would run smoothly at my second hearing, my mother arrived at Troup County on June 22, 1930. She had letters of introduction to a large number of prominent men and officials. She was confident that, owing to the vast amount of effort and the great number of people interested in my case, I would be speedily pardoned or paroled.

My mother's confidence was so great that I felt as though I were already freed.

CHAPTER XXI

The Serious Barrier Of Georgia Prejudice

M Y BROTHER, the Reverend Vincent Godfrey Burns, Pastor of Union Church, Palisade, New Jersey, arrived in Georgia on July 2 shortly after my mother's arrival. He brought with him all of the affidavits mentioned heretofore, and letters of introduction from some of the most influential persons and politicians of the East. Among them were: Franklin D. Roosevelt, Governor of the State of New York; Governor Larson, of the State of New Jersey; Ex-President Calvin Coolidge; George Gordon Battle, prominent New York lawyer; Congressman Randolph Perkins; Christian P. Paschen, Commissioner of the Department of Buildings, City of Chicago; Ex-Secretary of the Navy Josephus Daniels; John Fromm, Commander of the American Legion; Honorable Joab Banton, then District Attorney of New York County; Joseph F. Novotny, Commander of the American Legion of Cook County, Illinois; Charles J. Dodd, District Attorney of Kings County (Brooklyn), and a host of others.

He visited me at Troup County camp, accompanied by my mother, on July 4. He brought with him at this time the great mass of letters and affidavits that he had procured in my behalf. In looking over these documents I was greatly surprised to see a number of prominent Geogians who were agitating for my release.

Among the most prominent of them were: Senator Harris, Congressman Wright, Preston S. Arkwright, President of the Georgia Light & Power Company; Clint W. Hager, U. S. Attorney for the Northern District of Georgia; Andrew C. Erwin, Secretary of the Southern Mutual Insurance Company; Hunt Chipley, President of the Cumberland Bell Telephone Company; J. R. Holliday, and Bobby Jones, world's champion golfer, of Atlanta, Georgia; and his father, a prominent lawyer of the same city.

When you take into consideration the standing, integrity, and character of these people from many different states of the Union and add to it the hundred-odd sworn character affidavits from highly responsible and equally prominent people who were personally acquainted with me and vouched for my character, you would naturally draw the conclusion that my pardon or parole was simply a matter of legal formality.

This becomes more convincing when you take into consideration that I had conformed to the State law of Georgia which specifically stated that a convict is eligible for parole after twelve months of good conduct.

At last the day came for the hearing. Everyone in Troup County, all the prisoners and guards, were convinced that in a few more days I'd be on my way to Chicago, a free man.

The hearing was called to order by Chairman Rainey, but for some reason Commissioner Stanley was not present. The other commissioner, Judge G. A. Jones, a personal friend of Warden Hardy of Troup County, Attorney Schley Howard and my brother were the only persons present.

The total time allotted to this hearing was five minutes. The only spoken words were uttered by Attorney Howard who at this time was a special prosecutor appointed by Solicitor General John A. Boykin. Attorney Howard reiterated what he said at the first hearing: namely, that I had repaid the expenses of the State of Georgia, that I had been a model prisoner, and that I should be released in time to reclaim the position I had built for myself in Chicago.

He further stated that he had received information that the managers of my business could not continue without me after September first. This ended the hearing.

While there was no spoken opposition to my plea, Solicitor Boykin had written a letter to the Prison Commission, vigorously opposing clemency for the following reasons:

1. I was an escaped convict.

2. I hadn't made sufficient time.

3. My conduct after my escape was reprehensible.

This was vastly different from what he had said about me at my first hearing.

At that time I was a "menace to society—a continual and perpetual violator of the law." This statement of his was absolutely contrary to the truth. I challenge Mr. Boykin or any other officer of the law to produce any evidence of any conviction prior to my conviction in Georgia, or any conviction after my escape from Georgia.

Further, the sworn evidence from unquestionable and reliable sources which was in his possession at that time bore mute testimony that I was not a continual and perpetual violator of the law, as he so branded me in his letter to District Attorney Joab Banton of New York.

At the time Mr. Boykin wrote this letter, he never expected that his misrepresentation as contained in this letter would ever fall into my hands and enable me conclusively to prove that there was a deliberate underhand attempt to stamp me as a vicious criminal.

While everybody even remotely concerned with my case was emphatic in their assertions that I would soon be a free man, I still had my doubts. These doubts originated in my subconscious mind, and were supported by my mental analysis of the forces aligned against me and my surroundings.

Georgia is overloaded with traditions, sectional prejudices, and stubborn precedents. In mentally searching for the origin of these attributes, I applied my knowledge to account for their existence. Let me express in a few words the result of my mental observations which caused me to doubt the outcome.

Georgia suffered heavily in the Civil War. After the War, she was faced with the problem of reconstruction on a new social foundation. The people were poor, their wealth had been destroyed, there was nothing to tax and nothing to pay the taxes with. Many difficult problems demanded instant solution.

One of these problems was the disposition of convicted lawbreakers. There were no penitentiaries or workhouses. In the face of a rising tide of lawlessness the problem demanded an immediate solution. Georgia met the crisis with the prison contract system. It worked about as follows:

A man was convicted of a crime and sentenced, say, to three to five years. A prison contractor would appear at the county jail, look the man over, estimate his worth in terms of labor, and bid for his services at the rate, say, of twenty-five dollars a year. The State accepts the bid.

The contractor pays the State seventy-five dollars. He takes the hopeless victim away with him in chains to a condition worse than slavery, to the brutal prison camps operated for private profit in existence at that time.

If the victim is poor and friendless, he is confronted with three years of bitter misery. If the victim's family has any wealth or social standing at all, this is what would generally occur. Some member of the family would visit the prison contractor. They would discuss the situation. The contractor had invested seventy-five dollars in this prisoner. The contractor's only interest was profit. The result of the discussion would be that the victim's relatives would give the contractor the seventy-five dollars he had invested in this man and a substantial profit to boot.

The man would then be made a trusty, and given no duties at all and be virtually a free man, except that he would have to remain in the vicinity of the prison camp.

The next step would be to visit the Prison Commission. The relatives and the contractor would go together to see the members of this Commission. They would tell them what a model prisoner he was and that the ends of justice would best be served by granting him a parole.

The Prison Commissioners received an extremely moderate salary in view of their responsibilities and duties. They would also know by this visit that there was money in the air. A gratuity would be paid each of them by the prisoner's relatives and in a few weeks, the prisoner would be a free man.

This racket resulted in much public condemnation. The legislature, in attempting to remedy this condition, passed two amendments to the Georgia criminal statutes. One was that no convict would be entitled to parole until he had made twelve months in prison with good conduct. The other was that prisoners sentenced for life were not eligible for parole until they had been incarcerated three years.

Some time after 1900 the legislature of Georgia abolished the prison contract system, substituting the present system, which is simply an outgrowth of the old regime. Today, the county is the contractor. Although the county does not pay the State any money for the use of the convicts, they are compelled to clothe, feed, and house the prisoners at the county expense.

Paroles for convicts are not based upon the merits or justice of the convict's cause. His release is dependent upon the amount of local political influence his relatives can wield, or the payment of gratuities.

When the Georgia officials read this they may deny my allegations vigorously, admitting, perhaps, that this may have once been the case, but is not true today. My answer to that is stated in unequivocal terms: If they deny these allegations, I say they lie.

Now, get back to my case. The original arrangements on which I returned to the jurisdiction of the Georgia prison, where I was to get clemency, were based upon the fact that each of the three Prison Commissioners was to receive $500. This they never got. Five hundred dollars to these commissioners is a lot of money, as their salaries are scarcely more than those paid to a responsible clerk.

They looked forward to that $500 with great expectations, and were much chagrined when they didn't get it. If they would accept a gratuity to let me go, is it not possible that they would also accept a gratuity to keep me there?

Now, there is the matter of sectional tradition and prejudice which plays an important part in the scheme of things in Georgia. For some inexplicable reason Georgia has always been prejudiced against Catholics, Jews, Yankees and Negroes.

History will account for their prejudice against Yankees and Negroes, but even at this writing, I am at an utter loss to account for their religious intolerance. This sectional tradition and prejudice is not only directed against individuals, but also against cities, especially so against the cities of New York and Chicago. These are the two cities where I spent most of my life.

Their hatred of New York is found in direct expressions made to me by prisoners, guards, and free citizens while I was in Georgia, but I am not going to go into this further here because I believe it would only serve to stir up hatred. General accusations against myself, direct to me, and referring to all Northerners as well, were of an unprintable nature.

I sometimes wonder if, deep down in the heart of every Georgian, there is not a subconscious hatred of the Northerner. Sherman's March to the Sea was accompanied by unbelievable desolations and terrors. Perhaps some of the acts of the Union Army in that historic march may have been uncalled for, and unnecessary, for they left scars on the hearts of these people that three generations have not removed, and the consequence is that throughout the State this subconscious feeling is still struggling for expression.

If you were to visit Georgia and were arrested, accused of some violation of the law, the first question the Judge would ask you would be: "Where do you come from?" and the next, "What church do you go to?" If the answers to these questions brought out the fact that you were a Northern Catholic or a Jew, you would be in need of help.

CHAPTER XXII

Driven to Desperation

THE DAY of my second hearing had arrived and I had pondered all of the angles of my case. The known facts were these: The sworn testimony of over a hundred responsible persons who knew me personally, testifying to my good character and reformation—this testimony augmented by the powerful and political individuals mentioned heretofore, who had written to the officials requesting my release.

On the other hand, were the sworn affidavits of my wife, painting me as a criminal, but uncorroborated; the hazy, infinite intrigue from Chicago; the determined opposition of Boykin; the chagrin of the Prison Commissioners at not receiving the gratuities they expected; and the hosts of sectional traditions, prejudices, and precedents.

Which would win?

Regardless of the outcome, I had reached a definite and determined resolution. If I was not paroled, I would attempt to escape again, even though this attempt would result in death. For, to me, if I had to choose between calmly remaining in a Georgia chain gang for six, seven, or ten years, I would prefer the gamble with death. And if I lost, I would still be content, for perhaps death would free me from a future that if known would be worse than death.

I want the world to get this straight right here. While Georgia may say that I escaped from justice, I emphatically state that I am convinced that I escaped from injustice, intolerance and the vengeance of a society that is a hundred years behind the times.

Let the reader decide which is correct.

The day of the hearing had come and passed. It is customary for the Prison Commission to hear clemency cases on the first Monday of each month and to render their decisions to the Governor and the public about the twentieth or twenty-fifth of the same month.

On the third Sunday in July, my mother visited me at the camp. In a few days the commission would announce their decision. In the interval between the date of the hearing, July 9, and the third Sunday in July, my mother and brother had been extremely active among local political forces in trying to exert political pressure on the commission to decide in my favor.

On this day when she visited me my mother was telling me the results of her efforts. She was positive that there was no doubt of the outcome. I disagreed with her. She said:

"Elliott, do you mean to tell me that with all the facts, and the people working for you, that you still believe they won't let you go?"

"Yes," I replied.

Upon hearing this, she became greatly agitated and said: "Elliott, what will you do if they turn you down? I think they are trying to kill you and me, for if you have to stay here six or seven years more, it will kill me—of that I am sure."

"Mother," I said, "all is not lost. Courage and knowledge are all that are required to overcome any obstacle of life. I have a fair quantity of both and if I am turned down, I shall use both of these qualities to the utmost. I will escape again. I am preparing to put a plan of escape into action."

"But Elliott, you can't escape. You'll never get away with it. They will kill you surely; besides, there has been so much publicity about you. Every newspaper in the country has your picture, and you'll surely get caught."

"Mother," I said, "would you not rather see me dead, peacefully slumbering in some quiet, shady grave, knowing that my troubles were forever solved, than to know that I was going through the daily mental and physical torture of this damned chain gang and its visible horrors of injustice and intolerance? Regardless of what you and Vincent may think, I am going to try to escape if I am turned down."

The Prison Commission had rendered their verdict of the cases they had heard during the month of July, but had made no mention of mine. My petition for clemency had been tabled.

My mother, through inquiries, had not arrived at any definite conclusion as to when they would pass on my case.

I said to her: "Mother, you know and have been told that the Prison Commission is opposed to publicity. If I were a desperate criminal and it was an honor to society to keep me in prison, they would not be opposed to publicity, as such publicity would bring honor to their act. But because they know I am not a criminal and am entitled to clemency, they are afraid of publicity, as it compels them to explain a decision that is not substantiated by fact.

"The reason they withheld the decision was because they know that if they decide against me now, people will call upon them for an explanation, but by tabling my petition and postponing their decision, they will be gaining the distinct advantage of time, as the interest in my case will diminish as time goes on. This is the last Sunday you will be here, and I want to bid you goodbye. I want you to go home knowing that Georgia cannot win, for if they do not decide the case in my favor when they make their verdicts known for the month of August, I shall begin immediately some plan of escape.

"If I don't succeed, death will be the answer and your worries and my worries will be over in either case. And in either case, Georgia will lose."

We finally kissed each other goodbye and she told me that she would pray for me and ask God to watch over and care for me.

With a heavy heart I read the decisions of the Prison Commission for the month of August. They gave their decisions on cases heard that month. But still, there was no mention of mine. I was convinced that they were stalling for time, waiting for the interest to die down so that they could decide against me with as little unfavorable publicity and criticism as possible. Every prisoner in every penitentiary knows what time can do. As time goes by, he slowly becomes lost in the oblivion of forgotten men.

Was this happening to me?

There was only one person in the world who could prevent that coming to pass. That one person was myself. I had told my mother I would try to escape. I had dreamed that I would escape. The time had come when I should escape. Was I equal to the task? Did I have the courage?, Was I merely hypnotizing myself?

And what could I lose by trying? If I continued to stay; in prison the valuable business that I had built up would pass out of my hands anyway. The woman I loved I would never see again, and when my time was up, I would leave Georgia a beaten man with no place in society, and be compelled to start life over again, handicapped by my prison experience, ignorant of the changes that would have taken place in society while I was in prison.

What good would life be for me then? What I wanted, what I earned, what I deserved right now was freedom, while I still had the force, and character, and determination, to become an efficient, creative member of society. What I wanted was life, not living death.

I did have the courage. I visualized my contemplated act as follows:

If Death, in the personification of a being, should approach me with a cup of dice and say: "Burns, I'll gamble with you. One throw of the dice. If you win, you're free; if you lose, you die. Will you shake?"

"Would I shake? Bring on the dice!"

CHAPTER XXIII

Preparation for a Daring Break

SUCH WAS my feeling when I left the camp on the morning of September 1 to go to work in the vicinity of Mountville, Georgia, about seventy-five miles from Atlanta.

Right here let me explain that a part, and a very important part, of my plan to escape had already, at this point, been accomplished. Secreted in my clothes I had $150 in cash wrapped into a tight wad, the bills being in the following denominations: two fifties, four tens, and two fives. The reason for these particular denominations will become apparent to the reader a little later. As to how I secured this money and from whom—that I cannot tell. To do so would be betraying the person who helped me at a time when the obtaining of this money meant almost the difference between life and death to me.

It was a very hot day, and as we passed a small country store, I requested permission to buy some cold "dopes" for myself and the guard. My request was granted and one of the guards accompanied me into the store.

While making the purchase, the storekeeper discovered that I was the notorious bandit from Chicago who had made good, become wealthy and returned to the chain gang and was trying to get paroled. The storekeeper asked me what chances I thought I had of obtaining freedom. I told him frankly that I did not know. This storekeeper was an exception, however, and answered me as frankly, saying that he would like to see me free, as he thought the State of Georgia was doing me a grave injustice.

Sitting in a corner of the store was a man, a typical product of Georgia, dressed in overalls and cotton shirt and big straw hat, bronzed by years under the Georgia sun. I had not noticed him until he voluntarily spoke up:

"Gosh darn it, I'd like to see you get out, even if you are a Yankee. If I had an airplane, I'd take you off this chain gang and land you up the country and I know you'd pay me well."

Without directly looking at him, I glanced out of the corner of my eye and mentally fixed him in my mind for future identification.

I realized that he did not intend to say openly that he would take me off the chain gang, but I knew that he had spoken, without thinking, the thoughts that were in his subconscious mind, and that here was a man who needed money, because, thinking I was wealthy, he mentioned the fact that I would pay him well.

All of these thoughts went through my mind like a flash of lightning as I stood there in the store. I noticed that his statement went for what he meant it to be, merely a jest, by both the guard and the proprietor of the store.

Late that afternoon, while working on the road from Mountville, I glanced up from my work and noticed this same individual walking down the road toward where we were working. The guards had for some time been lulled into a sense of security by the fact that I had been in prison a year, and because I had always steadfastly maintained to them that I would never try to escape and would make every day of my time if Georgia demanded it. Because of the immense publicity given my case and the great number of natives who used to come to the place where we were working just to see me, the guards would overlook the violation of their speaking to me.

As he approached us, I maneuvered at my work to that side of the road on which he was walking so that he would be compelled to pass close to me as he went by us. Before he reached me, he stopped to speak to one of the guards.

After a few minutes he was beside me and I looked up at him.

"Hello," I said.

"Hello, yourself. How are you getting along?" he replied.

"Well, for a man in a chain gang, I'm getting along pretty good. But prison under any conditions is prison still. I noticed what you said in the store this morning about taking me off the chain gang in an airplane. While I know you haven't any airplane, I am sure that if I paid you well, you would help me escape."

Anticipating the possibilities of such a conversation with this man (whose name must never be known), I had extracted one of the fifty-dollar bills from its place of concealment while he was talking to the guard, and

128

had folded it into a small square in such a manner that the figure fifty would be on the outside and easily visible in the palm of my hand.

At this point of the conversation I let him catch a glimpse of the folded fifty-dollar bill by turning the palm of my hand wherein lay the folded bill, cupped in my palm in the manner employed by magicians.

Would he turn me in to the guard? And would the guard report the incident to the Warden? I would be severely punished for this overt act if betrayed.

Everything hinged on his reaction when he would see the money. Had my deductions been correct? Would fifty dollars tempt him?

It was with these thoughts running through my mind, and under a terrific tension, that I watched his reaction as he glanced at the money.

His eyes widened. He turned and looked at the guards, then looked directly at me with his mouth open in speechless astonishment, and he said to me:

"I am a poor man with a large family and I am in dire need of money. That fifty dollars would mean a great deal to me and I think you ought to be free. I don't know how I could help you, and while I won't betray you, I don't want to get into any trouble myself, for it means that I would be on the chain gang too."

"Have you got an automobile?"

"Yes."

"What kind is it and how fast can it run?"

I have to protect this man and so cannot name the make of the car, as it might be a means of identifying him. He told me that he had a coupe and it could make about forty miles an hour.

"That's the very thing," I told him, looking up to see if any one of the three guards was taking any special interest in my conversation with him. Since they had no occasion to consider it anything but a simple conversation of the type which had occurred many times before when curious natives known to them would stop to ask me a few questions, they paid no attention.

On the spur of the moment, standing there in the road, I evolved a plan which I hastily sketched to him.

I asked him if he could hide his automobile in the woods close by, indicating a large, black gum tree about 300 yards from the road. I told him that it would be necessary to have the car there between 7:30 and

8 o'clock on the following morning. I wanted him to drive me into the city of Atlanta about seventy-five miles away. Also, he would have to take some route to Atlanta that would enable him to pass around, instead of through, Newnan, as this was the only large city between where we were and Atlanta, as it was possible that after my escape was discovered, the prison officials would wire to Newnan authorities to be on the lookout.

In order that I would know that everything was in readiness, he was to conceal himself in the bushes between the hidden car and where I was working on the road, and give me the signal by imitating the whistle of a mockingbird.

This plan had been evolved and explained to him in much less time than it takes you to read it. He admitted that the plan was feasible and, if carried out according to schedule, should be successful.

There is an element involved here which both he and I understood perfectly, since I was on a chain gang and he had lived in Georgia all his life, which I shall explain now.

This element concerns the procedure taken by the warden and the guards when a convict takes to the bushes in a dash for liberty. Here is what happens:

If they see him going, they shoot at him with shotguns. If they miss him, they herd all the convicts of that group together to prevent a general break. Then, one of the guards sets out in a fast car for the camp to raise a general alarm. At the camp, they are always prepared for instant action in the event of an escape. The guard who has gone to the camp immediately returns to the scene of the escape, bringing with him the bloodhounds and some additional guards. The bloodhounds are immediately let loose on the fugitive's trail.

Simultaneously with the guard's departure from the camp, every available automobile (and several are always kept in readiness) at the camp, starts out at a swift pace to patrol the roads in the vicinity of the escape and, correlating with these actions, another guard at the camp begins to telephone to the sheriffs and police of all the nearby towns, describing the convict, and so forth, and organizing posses at strategic points in every direction.

In less than an hour's time, the countryside is swarming with armed guards and natives diligently searching for the escaped man. A reward of fifty dollars paid to whoever apprehends him, plus the attending honor of effecting the capture, spurs them on.

The convict has but two chances of success, the better one being to immediately get off the ground and into a fast-moving automobile. The only other chance he has is eluding the dogs and sticking to the woods.

You now have a picture of what happens when a convict escapes. If a convict gets into the bushes without being hit by the guards' shots, he has from thirty to forty minutes' start before the full machinery of the man-hunt swings into operation.

Under the plan that I presented there on the road, both he and I were well aware that we would be fifteen or twenty miles away before the hunt got into full swing.

I gave him another glance at the fifty-dollar bill and asked him if he was willing to try it on the morrow. After some hesitation, as though he was weighing something in his mind, he said:

"By Jove, I will! You have no idea how bad I need that money."

"Seven-thirty, then, tomorrow," I said.

"Between seven-thirty and eight," he answered, "be looking out for me."

"I sure will," I replied, and with this our conversation ended and he continued his journey down the road.

With great expectations, mingled with nervousness, already my whole consciousness becoming taut by the potent possibilities that would break forth with the dawn of a new day, I returned to my prison toil.

That evening I could not sleep. I went over again and again in my mind every detail of the plan and tried to anticipate every move of the prison officials. I even made definite plans as to every act and every move I would make if I got as far as Atlanta.

Late that night, out of sheer weariness, I dropped off into a sleep troubled by the realization that freedom or disaster loomed ahead. We were awakened as usual at 3:30 A.M. and I did not feel so well because of the lack of sleep and the nervous tension I was under.

Back on the road to Mountville at the scene of my contemplated break, I felt a whole lot better. All time is told by the sun. The convicts in Georgia prisons can always come within a few minutes of the time by noticing the size of the shadow cast by their bodies when they stand in a specific position facing the sun, their forms serving as human sun dials.

The zero hour had arrived. He had said "between seven-thirty and eight." My shadow told me that it was seven-thirty.

I waited with bated breath for the fatal signal.

Seven forty-five.

No signal as yet.

Every minute seemed like an hour. My muscles became taut and my mind grew heated.

Would he come?

Again I looked at my shadow. I knew it was 8 o'clock, or very near it.

CHAPTER XXIV

Another Try at Breaking the Gang

B UT NO signal yet. Was my deliverer coming?

Again I looked at my shadow.

It was 8 o'clock. Still no signal. Disappointment replaced hope.

My shadow said 8:10—and I knew that the man who had promised to aid me was not coming. The tension in my body and mind relaxed; hopelessness and despair settled over me. I continued my work, discouraged and baffled.

Later in the afternoon, whom should I see coming down the road, but my nameless friend! Again he stopped to talk with the guard, and again he walked up to me.

When he was close enough to me for a low-toned conversation, I spoke first, and said:

"Where the hell were you?"

"I couldn't make it this morning," he answered.

I saw at once that he wasn't so keen about the job. Hastily, I went over the plan again, using all of my powers of persuasion to sell him the idea, and increased the remuneration by five dollars. As we had moved down the road a little distance from where we had formulated our plan the day before, I indicated another landmark at which to hide the car.

My conversation with him revived his waning courage and he again promised to be there with his car on the following morning, the only change from the original plan being the new landmark, and the increase of payment from fifty to fifty-five dollars.

I passed the balance of the afternoon and night in the same mental condition as the day and evening previous.

The next morning, for the second time, I was eagerly awaiting the magic signal. My shadow indicated 7:45. The signal had not yet come. He had failed me once. It was very possible, I thought, that he would fail me again.

It was now 8 o'clock. Still no sign of him. What could be wrong?

Again bitter disappointment and despair. I began to wonder what could be this man's purpose in twice agreeing and twice failing to put in his appearance. Was he stalling for more money? Did he lack the courage? Was he planning to report me to the Warden? No matter how I analyzed these questions, I could arrive at no conclusive answer.

The day wore on. It was late in the afternoon. Looking up from my work, I saw my nameless friend coming down the road for the third time.

For the third time, he stopped a minute to talk with the guard. A few minutes later, we were engaged in conversation again. I spoke first:

"What the deuce are you trying to do, kid me?"

"No," he answered, "but I've got to be mighty careful, as you know darn well that if we should get caught, I'll be on the chain gang with you."

I realized, from this remark, that he still wasn't quite sold on the proposition, and that I would have to use all my powers of salesmanship to get him to give the plan a trial. I went over the whole plan again, showing him that with care and discretion we should certainly beat the posse into Atlanta and that, as Atlanta was a large city, strangers were neither unusual nor conspicuous. I also increased the remuneration to sixty dollars and, to add to his incentive, I faithfully promised him that I would send him by mail an additional hundred dollars if I should safely get up the country.

This arrangement pleased him, and after making me faithfully promise to be sure and mail him the additional hundred dollars, he positively agreed to go through with the plan on the following morning with one change: instead of taking me to Atlanta, he would take me to College Park, a small suburb about fifteen miles from Atlanta, where I could catch a trolley-car and ride into Atlanta.

I agreed to this change. *Had I realized what this change was going to mean, I would never have accepted it.*

We selected a new landmark at which to hide the car, made necessary by the progress of the work of the convicts, and he continued on his way, leaving me with a strong feeling that he would not fail me this time. Perhaps you can imagine the nervous strain I was under for the balance of that day.

That night I did not sleep a wink. I rolled and tossed on my cot all night, going over again and again every detail of my case, every detail of my plan of escape, and tried to foresee and forestall every conceivable obstacle.

As I sat in the mess hall the following morning, I let my eye travel over the assembled convicts there and wondered if any of the other convicts quietly eating breakfast with me, had also some secret plan of escape. What would some of those same convicts give to have the opportunity; and the gamble that was mine that morning.

Work commenced that morning on the Mountville Road the same as it always had. Everything was regular, serene, and calm. There were twenty-four convicts in our group. We were stretched out along the road for a distance of about 300 feet. At one end stood one guard, shotgun in arm. At the opposite end stood another guard. These guards faced one another and thus could view all of the convicts as they were engaged in their toil. The third guard patrolled the road between the two guards.

The road on which we were working was an ordinary dirt road about eighteen feet wide, running through a rolling, wooded country. On either side of the road, and extending about ten or twelve feet from it, were weeds and underbrush about two feet high. About twelve feet from the road the underbrush became higher and heavier and ended in a dense woodland thirty feet farther up.

This meant that there was a space of about forty to forty-five feet from where I stood in the road to the protecting cover of the woods. I would have to beat the guards' gunfire in bridging this gap from where I stood in the road to the shelter of these woods.

The landmark this time was an extremely tall pine tree 300 yards away.

It was sometime after 5 o'clock when we commenced work that morning, and 7:30 was upon us before I realized it. This interval seemed to sweep upon me with a sudden swiftness, out of all proportion to the usual lapse of time. My shadow told me it was approximately 7:40.

My heart was beating like a trip-hammer as I awaited the signal that I knew was coming. In a second I heard the faint whistle of the mocking bird. It was repeated.

Casually I looked in the direction from which it came and noticed through the heavy foliage of the trees my nameless stranger, silently beckoning to me with his fingers.

The zero hour had struck.

I straightened up from my work as if to rest for a moment, and looked ahead at the guard standing at the end of the road. He seemed languid and unconcerned. I turned my body and looked at the guard at the other end of the road. He was talking to a convict near him. The third guard was behind me and walking toward the guard in front of me.

I would have to let a few seconds go by until the third guard had passed me in patrolling his beat; and while his back was to me, as he continued his course, I would make my dash.

He passed me. I dropped my shovel. Like a panther, I sprang at full speed toward the sheltering woods where my friend awaited me.

As I fled, the Negro beside me cried out: "*Man gone.*"

The startled guards were confused for a few seconds, the precious seconds that I needed. I was in the woods before they could bring their shotguns to a firing position in their excitement.

My nameless friend and I had arranged on the previous afternoon where I was to ride in the automobile. His car was a small coupe with a rumble seat. He had removed the rumble seat to make a compartment for transporting vegetables and watermelons from his farm to the nearby town of La Grange. It was in this compartment that I was to ride. Being very short in stature, he was sure that I could fit in it.

To provide ventilation, he was to place a small block of wood in between the lid and the frame. This would allow a narrow opening through which air could circulate and still present the appearance of being closed.

At the instant that I left the road, he started for the car. I followed him to the place where the car was parked, not far from a seldom-used wagon path that ran through the woods.

Since I ran the faster, we reached the car almost simultaneously. The motor was running. The rumble seat was open. But I stopped short in my tracks with a mingled feeling of surprise and fear as I saw a second stranger standing beside the car, with a large horse pistol in his hand.

What did this mean? Who was he?

I looked at my friend in speechless astonishment. He read the question in my face and said:

"Oh, he's all right. He's a friend of mine. Don't stop to ask questions. Get in and let's get going."

Without a word, I jumped in the compartment, the lid was closed, the block of wood inserted, and we were off. I was crouched in the semi-darkness in a contorted position and was shaken considerably as the car in its speed bumped over the rough and uneven ground. In about ten or fifteen minutes, by the smoothness of the motion of the car as its motor purred with a rhythm that was music to my ears, I could tell that we were on some highway, sailing along at forty miles an hour—to freedom.

So far, so good. The next step would be to procure clothes, as I was dressed in prison garb. Calling softly to my friend on the seat above me, I said:

"When you get a little farther on at some convenient place I want you to stop at a store and buy me a pair of overalls, size thirty, and a blue shirt, size fourteen."

"I guess we'll have time to stop at some store as we pass, to buy what you need," he said. "But we'll need some money to buy it with."

"All right," I replied.

With much difficulty, in my cramped position, I extracted a five-dollar bill, pushed the lid up gently and he reached back through the broken celluloid of the rear curtain and took the money.

We had been traveling without a break for about an hour when the car stopped, and he sent his companion into a store to buy me my overalls and shirt. I could not see where we were, but I could hear other people talking, as I lay concealed in my hiding place. After three or four minutes, which seemed an age to me, his friend came out of the store, got back into the car and said that he could not get anything near my size in shirt or overalls in that store.

The car started and we were on our way once more.

We made several more stops trying to purchase the needed clothes. Finally they decided to give up getting my exact size and get the best they could at the next store. So at the next stop they secured a suit of overalls, size thirty-three, and a fifteen-and-a-half size shirt.

At this store they filled the radiator with water and set out once more at top speed. What direction they took or what roads they traversed, I will never know, but when we were within about six miles of College Park, they pulled off the highway and into a woods nearby. They stopped the car, got out, lifted up the lid, and said to me:

"Here's where we make the change."

As I climbed out of the car I noticed that his friend had the pistol in his hand, and I realized why he was there. This man's part was to be played in event that I didn't come across with the dough as promised.

"And we collect," they continued, "our money."

Reaching into the front of my shirt where I had the money concealed in a small tobacco bag suspended on a string around my neck, I withdrew sixty dollars and handed it to them. I then undressed, put on the shirt and overalls which were far too big for me. While I was putting on the overalls and shirt, they hid the convict's uniform in the bushes. After I had properly adjusted the overalls, we all climbed into the front seat and, with me sitting in between them, we continued our journey once more.

In a few minutes the car rolled into College Park. As we came to a stop at the end of the trolley line, I noticed with a flash of fear, the convicts of that county working nearby.

College Park is in Campbell County—the same county I had run away from eight years before and the one I came back to upon my return. I had been there five weeks before my transfer to Troup County. All of the guards, and some of the prisoners knew me by sight.

Also, out of curiosity, many of the residents of College Park had come to the camp in Campbell County on Sundays to see me when I first returned. I could not leave the automobile here. I informed my friend of this new danger, but he was adamant. He would not take me to Atlanta, and he would not go any farther. He had made a deal, and he was carrying it out to the letter.

Instantly, I realized that it had been my fault since I had not thought of this peril before.

The trolley-cars at College Park run every fifteen minutes. There was none in sight. I needed a shave; so in a flash, an idea came to me. I would leave the car, go directly into a barber shop that I saw nearby, and get a shave while waiting for the car. This would serve two purposes and would give me a place of shelter until the trolley-car arrived.

Bidding my deliverer goodbye and thanking him, I got out of the car and walked to the barber shop. There I got another shock; for the barber, whom I recognized instantly, was a deacon of the church that conducted services at the Campbell County camp when I was there the year previous. He had spoken to me several times and had sympathized with my cause. But I was already in the shop and I could not very well turn back.

CHAPTER XXV

Almost Recaptured

A GREAT surge of fear swept over me. Fighting desperately to get a grip on my nerves, I could do nothing but get in the chair—and take the desperate gamble that he might not recognize me.

I also realized that I must speak as little as possible, for my hated Yankee accent would be instantly recognizable to a native of Georgia.

I got in the chair and simply said, "Shave."

Apparently he failed to recognize me. He began his work and also attempted to open a conversation with me: but I affected lack of interest and maintained a stony silence.

While he was shaving me, several men came in and sat down. I could not see them because of my position in the barber chair. The barber commenced a casual conversation with them. While he was progressing with the shave, I was wondering who these men were, if they knew me and whether they were waiting to be shaved or whether someone had recognized me as I got out of the coupe and was casually waiting to arrest me.

Like all Southerners, the barber was infinitely slow and his apparent serenity convinced me after a while that there was no danger from the strange men with whom he was talking.

But while he continued to shave me the trolley-car from Atlanta that runs every fifteen minutes had come and gone. This would mean another fifteen-minute exposure to the possibility of recognition by some one who might accidentally come along while I waited for the next car.

The barber finally got through. I paid him and went out. Standing in front of the shop I could see the Campbell County convicts working on a new road but 300 feet away. At that distance I recognized one of the prisoners and the guards. It was now about 10:30 A.M. and quite a few people were on the narrow main street of College Park.

I couldn't wait for the car there, that was a cinch. I would have to do something and do it quick. I took the only course open to me, which was to walk up along the car tracks toward Atlanta to the next stop of the trolley-car, which would be indicated by a band of white painted on the trolley pole.

The stops are far apart and I would have to take a chance on reaching the next stop in time to catch the next car. Luckily, I made it.

Getting on the car I was aware of a new danger. Everybody that would be on the car at that point would be a resident of College Park and there would be a grave possibility of some one of the passengers recognizing me. However I took the bull by the horns and walked into the car.

The car reached Atlanta without incident.

Since my overalls and shirt did not fit me I would have to procure new clothes. I asked a newsboy in what part of the city the second-hand clothing stores were located.

"On Decatur Street," he replied.

I didn't know where Decatur Street was and upon my request he gave me directions. Reaching Decatur Street, I entered the first store that I saw. Speaking to the man who came forward as I entered, I said:

"I want a second-hand suit of clothes and I will not pay over ten dollars for it."

"We have no second-hand clothes here," he said, "but we have got some ten-dollar suits."

I selected a suit, the coat of which fitted me okay, but the pants were six inches too long and about three inches too big at the waist. I asked him if he would make the necessary alterations.

"We don't make alterations here," he said, "but if you wish to come around the corner to a little tailor shop with me, I'll fix you up. The alterations are extra, however."

"All right," I agreed.

I then bought a suit of underwear, a white shirt, a soft hat, a tie, a pair of socks and a dollar suit-case. I took all these purchases with me and went around the corner to the little tailor shop.

While the tailor made the alterations we both sat in his shop. The alterations completed, I changed clothes there, but upon putting on the pants, I discovered that he had not taken them in at the waist. Not wishing to delay any longer, we took in the slack by a simple expedient of pulling it together at the back and fastening it with a heavy safety pin on the inside. This done and my overalls and shirt of the early morning deposited in the cheap suit-case, we went back to the first store.

This was made necessary because I handed the salesman the other fifty-dollar bill in payment for the articles I had purchased, which totalled $14.95. We went back to the store together to get the change. The owner of the store was much surprised when his salesman handed him the fifty and refused to make change until he sent the bill to the bank to see if it was good. I had to wait there fully fifteen minutes until the man returned from the bank with the change.

Immediately on leaving the store, I stopped at a shoe-shine parlor and had my prison shoes cleaned and shined. With this last trace of prison life removed, I stepped out on the street carrying the suit-case and appearing to the casual passerby as an ordinary citizen.

I now had to get out of Georgia as swiftly as possible. I was positive that the police of Atlanta had already been advised of my escape by wire, but they had no definite reason to suspect that I went direct to Atlanta, as the Alabama State Line was only fifteen miles from where I made my break, and it was entirely probable that they might surmise that I was attempting to reach Montgomery or Birmingham.

With this thought in mind, I boldly inquired the direction of the railway terminal. Of course, there were plenty of pictures of me in Atlanta and while the majority of the police did not know me by sight, it was possible that they might recognize me from my photographs. However, this did not worry me so much for it was part of the game.

I reached the station and was about to go in when I stopped to analyze the full import of this move. It was highly probable that I could buy a ticket to some distant point and get on the train unmolested. But, on the other hand, once on the train, there was the possibility that my trail would be picked up and the news flashed ahead by wire to intercept me.

If I left Georgia by train from this terminal, I would be compelled to buy a ticket for Washington, D. C., to get out of Dixie, and as it would take over fifteen hours for the train to reach Washington, sufficient time would have elapsed to give the police a chance to pick up my trail.

Thinking this over, I abandoned the idea of leaving by train and asked the direction to the bus station. I arrived at the bus station a little before noon. I boldly entered and asked the attendant when the next bus left for Chattanooga, Tennessee. He told me the next one left at 1:10.

I checked my grip, bought a ticket for Chattanooga and went next-door to a restaurant, purchasing the early afternoon edition of a news-paper on the way. While eating the first decent meal I had tasted in fourteen months, I looked through the newspaper to see if my escape had become public knowledge as yet. There was nothing there.

I finished my meal by 12:30 and still had forty minutes until the time the bus would leave. Not caring to risk possible recognition by leaving the restaurant, I remained there drinking one glass of iced tea after another, as the day was very hot and the tea very soothing to my nerves.

I left the restaurant at six minutes after one by the clock on the wall. I knew that there would be a plainclothes man stationed at the bus terminal when the bus pulled out. This is a matter of police routine of which I had advance knowledge, and to pass him was the risk that I must take. I felt no unnecessary fear, however, because he meets all incoming and outgoing buses and probably had been assigned to that duty since 8 o'clock that morning and had not yet been advised of my escape.

The bus pulled in and I got on, choosing a seat by the window. In a minute or two it was on its way.

An hour later, with my coat off, sitting back comfortably in my seat, enjoying the cool breeze created by the speed of the bus, I was leaving Georgia at the rate of forty miles an hour. I was free once more. I had beat them again.

How beautiful the world looked. How enjoyable it was to sit back in comfort, enjoying the luxury and freedom of having no one observing my every move. Free! It is utterly impossible to put in language the magic influence that that one word—free—can mean to anyone after fourteen months of prison life.

While I was thus egotistically complimenting myself on my accomplishment of the morning, every revolution of the wheels was speeding me toward an unknown and unforeseen danger.

At about 4 o'clock the bus pulled into Rome, Georgia, and stopped at the bus terminal. The driver announced:

"We stop here for twenty minutes' rest. Rest rooms are in the station and refreshments can be bought nearby."

At this announcement, everyone in the bus, except me, got up to leave and take advantage of these few minutes to relieve the tedium of their journey. I elected to remain sitting in the bus, as I thought this was my safest course. But as the last person was stepping out of the bus, I noticed two typical Georgia sheriffs, in shirt sleeves and suspenders, carrying revolvers openly displayed on their hips, looking over each occupant of the bus as he stepped out onto the sidewalk.

Instantly, like a wild animal, I sensed this unexpected danger. My heart jumped violently and I was panic-stricken with fear. "The wires must be hot and these sheriffs are looking for me. I can't stay in the bus. What shall I do?" I thought wildly.

After the first wave of fear passed over me, I knew that I had to act instantly and, summoning up my courage, I got up and as calmly as possible walked out of the bus.

The sheriffs had spoken to no one as yet. I was fifteen or twenty seconds behind the last person to leave the bus and as I stepped out onto the street the sheriffs' eyes seemed to bore holes right through me and one of them, speaking to me, said:

"Where did this bus come from?"

The minute he said that to me, I knew he was looking for me, as he knew where that bus came from as well as I did. It was a pretext on his part, as there must have been some doubt in his mind that I was the man he sought. I realized all this even before his voice had died away.

Now had come my supreme test. Nothing but courage would save me now. Facing him as coolly as possible, I answered with one word: "Atlanta," and started to walk down the street.

CHAPTER XXVI

Out of Georgia to an Unknown Destination

TWENTY-FIVE or thirty feet ahead of me, I noticed a drug store and, anxious to get out of their sight, as I realized that if I would be out of their sight I would be out of their minds, I started to walk slowly toward it. Without looking back, I entered the drug store.

It was a typical drug store with an "L"-shaped soda counter on one side and a cigar counter and cashier on the opposite side. Entering the store, I walked up to the short part of the soda counter that runs parallel to the street and ordered a chocolate malted milk. While I was standing there waiting to be served, in walked the two sheriffs behind me.

They walked to the opposite end of the counter facing me and looked directly at me. I was panic-stricken and I strove desperately with every ounce of my nervous energy to control the muscles of my face so that they would not register the fear that was racking my body. The perspiration broke out on me in great drops. In a second or two I was wringing wet.

I must get away from the steady, direct gaze of their eyes which was shattering my nervous system, so I changed my position at the counter by walking around to the center of it. This placed me even closer to the sheriffs and gave them a profile view of me, but I was not compelled to look directly at them.

This act, I reasoned, would help me gain control of myself. The clerk deposited the malted milk in front of me and placed the check beside me. I had forgotten all about the malted milk and looked at it in horror as I instinctively knew that at that time I couldn't pick it up to drink it without my hand trembling as though I had the palsy.

Without turning my head to look at the sheriffs, I knew that they were still watching me, debating in their minds whether I was their man or not. I must, I decided, pick up that glass and drink, and I must do it in a way that would disarm the sheriffs.

My left hand and left side were toward the sheriffs. Summoning all my strength and attempting to mesmerize myself like the Hindoo priests of

India, I slowly closed the fingers of my right hand (which, of course, the sheriffs could not see) and clenched my fist with all my strength, which movement tightens up every muscle in the hand and arm, and slowly brought my closed fist up toward the glass. This act gave me complete control over all the muscles in the right hand and arm.

Boldly taking hold of the silver handle of the glass, I again closed my fist tightly around it and slowly lifted the glass to my lips steadily and calmly. Finishing the drink, I picked up the check, walked over to the cashier at the cigar counter, paid the check and walked out. All this was done calmly without one trace of hurry.

Once in the street, without looking back, I walked toward the bus station, deciding to enter it and spend the remainder of the time in the men's rest room. As I turned into the bus station, I noticed out of the corner of my eye, that the two sheriffs were standing in front of the drug store looking in my direction.

But somehow or other, my intuition told me that they had about decided that I was not their man. Then I heard the driver's welcome announcement, "All aboard!" and, in getting back in the bus with the other passengers, I could still see the sheriffs in front of the drug store. In a minute or so we were again on our way and the crisis was over.

What saved me was the fact that I had bought all new clothes; had been freshly shaved; the manner in which I had answered their question and my seemingly cool conduct while under their close scrutiny. *I hope they read this, as the laugh is on them.*

Once more the bus was swiftly on its way, but I learned from this incident that I must keep a cautious and vigilant outlook. I still had a long journey ahead of me.

The bus reached Chattanooga at 7:30 P.M. which was the terminus of that line. Going into the station, I inquired of the clerk when the next bus would leave for Louisville. Consulting a time-table, he told me it would not leave until 1:30 the next morning.

Here was another element of danger. Chattanooga is a small city and the streets are almost deserted by 10:30 at night. Anyone seen hanging around the streets at a late hour is very liable to be questioned by the police, and because of my experience at Rome, I was on guard.

I checked my suitcase in one of those new-fangled lockers which I noticed in the station, put the key in my pocket and went into a restaurant to get some supper and to think over how and where I would pass the time until the bus was ready to leave.

I had finished my supper by 8 o'clock, but the problem of what I would do between then and when the bus left, was still unsolved. While aimlessly walking back to the bus station, I noticed a hotel directly across the street from it. This gave me an idea.

Entering the hotel, I engaged a dollar room for the night, registered and paid the clerk, but did not even go up to look at the room, as I did not want to create suspicion by engaging a room without baggage. I walked across the street and into the bus station, intending to get my grip and go back into the hotel to take a much-needed rest and leave early the next morning on a later bus.

As I entered the station, I noticed that three or four employees were all grouped around the clerk who was telephoning. While I was inserting the key in the lock, I overheard the clerk say:

"So you say he escaped from La Grange this morning and he's a short stocky-built man about five-foot-four, and a hundred and twenty-five or thirty pounds . . ."

The clerk was repeating to those about him the message which he was receiving over the wire from some unknown source in a manner similar to someone describing a horse race or a baseball game over the telephone to a group of listeners.

What a break for me, that I, out of pure chance, should have walked in at this psychological moment. As there was no one present but employees, I took my grip and walked out of the station unnoticed because of their excitement and interest in the telephone message.

On reaching the street I walked rapidly away from the station, and also the hotel, my one thought being to get away from that vicinity. After walking a couple of blocks, I tried to figure out this new angle. The Georgia authorities were surely making a strenuous effort to intercept me, and I'd have to get out of Chattanooga some way that night.

Without any definite plan in view, I entered the lobby of a large hotel, checked my grip and sat down for a few minutes to try to figure out what my next move would be. I could not decide on any plan. Had the Georgia authorities also telephoned to the railway stations? Or had they definitely picked up my trail on the bus and perhaps learned only too late that because of the sheriffs' indecision at Rome, I had slipped through their fingers and that they expected to nab me at the bus station at Chattanooga?

Arriving at this decision, I entered the telephone booth and called up the railroad station. The next train was the Royal Palm which was a solid Pullman train traveling from Jacksonville, Florida to Cincinnati, Ohio. It would leave Chattanooga at 10:35, but as all the Pullman reservations were already occupied and several tickets already sold from Chattanooga to Cincinnati, they would add a day coach to the train. The fare was $12.85, and the train would arrive in Cincinnati at 8 o'clock the next morning.

I decided to take this train at all costs. To divert suspicion, I planned to take a taxicab to the station and tip the taxi driver profusely and have him carry my grip in the station for me to create the impression that I was somebody who traveled in style.

Going out on the street in front of the hotel I engaged in conversation with a taxi driver, as I did not know how far away the station was. I learned from him that it was but a few blocks away and that it could be reached in five minutes. I re-entered the lobby of the hotel to pass away a couple of hours between then and train time.

There I met a traveling salesman and we passed away the time playing rummy. I handed him a line that I was traveling for a New York wholesale house.

On the minute of 10:30, I left the hotel with my grip, got in a taxi and went to the station. I was a little nervous while purchasing my ticket and passing through the gate, as I thought I recognized a couple of bulls who were stationed there as a matter of routine. The train was a little late, but it finally got under way.

While sitting in the speeding train, I began to feel secure once more, as I knew that once safely arrived in Cincinnati, I would have reached the outer circumference of the widening circle of Georgia's sphere of influence, and the limits of the territory wherein they would have hoped to intercept me.

I was completely played out by the strenuous events of the day and, having had no rest the night before, I fell asleep.

I awoke by force of habit around 4 o'clock the next morning. After being awake an hour or so, I began to consider that there was a grave element of danger in leaving the railway depot at Cincinnati. I figured this danger out for three different reasons.

The most grave of these would be the construction of the depot in Cincinnati. I had been there before on numerous occasions and knew exactly how it was built. No train passes through Cincinnati. Incoming trains are backed into the station and the passengers are compelled to leave through an iron-barred enclosure almost similar to the entrance or exit of a penitentiary or jail.

As the passengers, in single file, pass out this gate, they can be subjected to a close scrutiny by a policeman or detective, if one should be stationed there. As a matter of police routine, I was sure a Cincinnati detective would be stationed there.

It was highly possible that Georgia officials had communicated with the Cincinnati police to be on the lookout for me, and so the policeman regularly stationed there might be watching for me, as this train pulled in, because he would have known that it came from Chattanooga.

There was another possibility that the newspapers of Cincinnati had already published the news of my escape and, perhaps, had a picture of me in their morgue from the year previous, which would enable an alert detective who had already read the paper to recognize and arrest me on his own initiative.

Sitting there in the day coach a little before dawn, I began to rack my brain for some way or method by which I could leave the station at Cincinnati without creating a trace of suspicion.

With the problem unsolved, I looked over the other passengers in the train. There were only three besides myself. Two of them were men and they were both asleep. The third was a stout buxom young lady about twenty-two years old and she was awake. Crowded beside her on the seat and in the rack over her head and in the seat opposite, were numerous grips and hat boxes. This gave me an idea.

If I could strike up an acquaintance with her, perhaps I could leave the depot with her, helping her carry some of her baggage and, to all appearances, journeying with her. This looked like a good way out. It would require tact to become sufficiently friendly with her to do this, but I decided to try.

I walked by her a couple of times on the pretext of getting a drink of water, to catch her eye, and finally I went boldly up, spoke, and sat down beside her. I made the grade. We became very chummy and I learned that the young lady came from a town in Georgia not far from where I had worked on the chain gang.

She was *en route* to Chicago to matriculate at a school near that city, and was anticipating with great enthusiasm her forthcoming educational opportunities. She was very well educated and I really enjoyed the three hours I spent with her on the train that morning.

Emboldened by my good fortune in making her acquaintance, as I knew already that it was a foregone conclusion that I would pass through the gate with her, helping her carry her baggage, I decided to go one step farther.

The train on which we were riding would arrive in Cincinnati about 8:15. She would change cars there and connect with the Big Four Railroad to continue her journey to Chicago. But, as the Big Four did not leave until a quarter of ten, she would have two hours to wait. These facts I learned during our conversation.

I had previously decided that upon reaching Cincinnati I would go to some hotel and secure a room for a day in which to bathe and rest before continuing my journey. Having no way of knowing at that time whether the Cincinnati papers would have any news of my escape, there would be danger in my registering at a hotel if the news had been published, because sometimes hotel dicks are even more curious than the regular police.

It would be a perfect cover for me if this girl beside me would accompany me to the hotel with her bag and baggage and register with me as my wife. If she would do this it would allay all suspicion.

When she had questioned me about myself, I had given her a false name and had told her that I was a traveling salesman and that I was going to stop at Cincinnati for two days. I had told her also that I was going to register at the—and that if she cared to accompany me she could take a bath and change her clothes, as she had previously indicated she would like to do, for she had been riding since 10 A.M. the day before.

At first she demurred, but when I convinced her that I would leave her in full possession of the room, allowing her enough time to bathe and change clothes, she finally consented.

The train arrived at Cincinnati. I walked out through the iron gate, nonchalantly carrying her bag and baggage, and with her beside me. We took a taxi to the — Hotel where I registered and we went to our room. I went out to get breakfast and to purchase editions of all the newspapers in Cincinnati, while she took a bath and changed her clothes.

When it came time for her to leave, I took her to the station and bade her goodbye. Should the young lady in question read this story, she will be greatly surprised to learn that, unknown to her, she aided a convict who escaped from her own State.

Leaving her at the station, I returned to the hotel for a much-needed bath and sleep. I woke up about 5 o'clock and purchased a ticket on a bus to a distant point. The bus left Cincinnati about 5.30 P.M.

That night, while approaching Columbus, Ohio, I fell into conversation with an elderly woman sitting in the seat next to me. She was discussing the fire that had occurred at Ohio Penitentiary a few months before. She was telling me how she had visited the prison a few weeks before the fire. The terrible loss of life that occurred there depressed her, and she could not account for man's brutal inhumanity to man.

In discussing the convicts, she said: "They are just human beings like you and me."

I smiled to myself and thought: "I wonder what she'd say if she thought she was sitting next to an escaped convict."

We arrived at Columbus a little after midnight and got out for half an hour's rest. I entered the bus station which was a combination restaurant and waiting-room. So far, in my journey, I was ahead of the newspapers, not having seen any account of my escape. The first thing I did on entering the restaurant was to purchase all editions of the Columbus papers, and there, staring me in the face, on the front page of each one of them were headlines, one reading: "Famous Robber Escapes Again"; another "Chicago Editor Makes Second Escape"; and the third, "Famous $4 Bandit Beats Georgia Pen Twice."

The restaurant was full of people, some from my bus and some from other buses, and while they were eating their sandwiches, everybody began talking about me. One of the papers had a one-column picture of me, but it was not very good. I kept to myself, as I ate my sandwiches and drank my coffee, and was glad to hear the driver say "All aboard!"

No one in the restaurant recognized me from my picture and I got on the bus to continue my journey to a destination that forever must remain unknown.

Unknown then, unknown now—a fugitive running the gauntlet of police wherever I go, expecting any minute to feel the clutching hand of legal vengeance upon my shoulder. A fugitive . . . not from justice but from injustice.

151

Eighteen months ago I was a respected citizen. Founder and active head of a flourishing publishing business. A lecturer on educational and inspirational subjects. A creative force in society. Happy . . . working for the common good . . . inspired by the love of a good and beautiful woman . . . I had everything that a man can desire.

Those achievements were acquired by seven years of hard, honest, industrious work, and now—a fugitive. In the lapse of time, I have committed no crime, I have broken no laws . . . and yet . . . all that is swept away. Separated from my family and friends and the woman I love, I am compelled to start life anew, unknown, in a strange place.

CHAPTER XXVII

A Fugitive in his Native Land

I AM STILL a fugitive!

Many people no doubt wonder what were my feelings as I put aside the prison garb, I hope forever, and again began to take up civilized life. How have I kept my identity a secret and why *must* I keep it a secret?

Here is what actually happened! And in this account I am going to give the simple facts and even the names of the places where I have been.

My destination on that bus was Pittsburgh, Pennsylvania!

Before making my escape from Georgia I had figured out one way by which I could conceal my identity. John Pashley, a buddy of mine in the gang, was exactly my height, build and complexion. He had a card from the merchant marine certifying him as a first-class seaman and giving the particulars as to his personality. These particulars fitted me also. When his time was nearly up and he was about to leave the gang he showed me this card and, as one last favor, I begged him for it. He gave it to me, and with this card in my pocket I considered myself fairly safe, for if someone suspected me of being Robert Burns, the famous four-dollar bandit, I could show him the card and pass as my convict friend, John Pashley.

I arrived safely in Pittsburgh without incident, and there boarded a bus for Newark, New Jersey!

I was making my way to the state of New Jersey for one and only one reason. My brother is a minister there, and intimately connected with many powerful friends in the state. He had previously told me that if I ever escaped again I was to come to him and he would help me.

And let me say this right here. My mother and my brother have been my staunch friends and supporters through all the misfortunes that have befallen me during the last thirteen years since the war.

I alternately read the newspaper and dozed as the bus made its course through the valleys and across the quiet farm country of Pennsylvania. As I passed through many a quiet hamlet and watched the simple farm people go their way, I thought how little they knew of the world with its pangs and sufferings and sin.

The sun set, night came on and in darkness we were finally arriving at our destination. The overland bus was approaching the city of Newark. It was now late at night and in the distance could be seen the myriad lights of the many tall buildings.

Men and women who have been riding all day and night in silence are beginning to arouse themselves. The long journey is coming to an end, and conversations between fellow-travelers begin here and there. Some are soon to be among friends and loved ones. Some will soon be at home. Others, perhaps, will only be strangers in a strange land. Some are anticipating joy and happiness. Others only sorrow and gloom, trying to lose their unhappiness in the byways of a great city, running away from life. Who would imagine that perchance some one in that bus might be running away from the law; that I, an escaped convict, was planning to lose myself in the teeming millions of the great metropolis?

"We'll reach the city about 4:30 A.M.," volunteered the man next to me, "Four-thirty on a Sunday morning, so I guess I'll go to a speak-easy for a few beers and wait until the town's awake. Want to come along with me?"

"Is there no other place to go?" I asked.

"Only speak-easies and all-night restaurants."

"Thanks, I'll try a restaurant."

An hour later I was sitting in Silver's restaurant, sipping a cup of coffee. Next to me sat a man scanning the Sunday edition of a metropolitan newspaper. He was having a bite before retiring late from an early party.

"Pardon me," I asked, addressing the late reveller, "can you tell me how to go to_____?"

"Sure" (and he gave me complete directions). "By the way," he continued, "I see that Chicago editor escaped from the chain gang again. I'm glad to see him get away. They should have let him go in the first place, after he made good. I can't see the justice in keeping him in prison. He doesn't look like a criminal to me. What do you think?" and the speaker pointed to a photograph of me on the open page.

Sitting there beside him I glanced at my own photograph and the newspaper account of my second escape and answered, "I don't read the newspapers much and so I know very little about it." My heart was missing beats, and I wished that I had gone with the stranger on the bus for a few beers.

The photograph was a poor one, and the man was tired, so he never gave a thought that he might be talking to the man referred to in the newspaper. Such is life. That I might be sitting there next to him would be *too* incredible. In a few seconds he had turned the page and was absorbed in other events of a world overflowing with tragedy, drama, and comedy.

At 9 o'clock that Sunday morning I was walking down a pretty suburban street lined with shady trees and cozy homes in___, New Jersey. I was searching for a certain house. I had never been in ____ before. I had never seen this house. In the house for which I was looking lived a friend whom I could trust. I needed a friend now. With only $1.80 left and the telegraph wires buzzing in police stations and newspaper offices advising an astounded world of my second escape, I needed money and a place to hide.

I was sure my friend would loan me some money and would help me in this critical hour of need.

Finding the house at last, I rang the bell. No answer. Again and again I rang—still no answer. With a sinking heart I noticed the mail box; it was filled with an accumulation of mail. My friend was not home, away for the week-end perhaps. "Maybe he will be home by evening," I thought, "so I'll go out into the country and wait until dusk."

That evening when I returned, the house was dark, the mail still there.

Worried and deeply disappointed, I walked aimlessly away. In Massachusetts lived my mother—the truest, best mother God ever gave a son. But she might just as well have lived at the North Pole. One dollar and eighty cents would not bridge the gap from where I was to where she lived. What should I do? Where should I go? As fast as train and bus could carry me for two days I had speeded here, and now my friend was not at home and might be away for several days. Oh! if I had only gone to my mother's house instead. And so I mused, as I wandered from street to street, sleepy, tired and in despair.

Quick thinking and courage born of daring are powerful weapons. As I walked I thought, "I *must* not be caught. I must act. I must act *now—this* very minute. I will." I did.

A little later I was in the railroad station in Hackensack, N. J. I called my mother on the long distance phone, reversing the charges. The connection was made, and the person who answered told me she was out and would not be home until after 10:30 P.M. "Tell her to phone (giving the number of the public phone I was using) at 11 o'clock tonight and that R. E. B. (giving my initials only) will be waiting for her call."

That was taking a long chance, for I did not know to whom I was speaking, and there was grave possibility that my mother's home was under surveillance.

At five minutes to eleven I was back in the railroad station, nervously watching a certain phone booth. It was a desperate chance, but I was desperate too. At eleven the phone rang. It was my mother and my brother was visiting her. I spoke to my brother. In a few words I told him of my plight. He would mail me $25.00 addressed to John Smith, general delivery, right away. It would reach Hackensack (name of town I was in) Monday afternoon.

Monday afternoon I called at the post office. Yes, there was a letter for John Smith. "Nice day," said the clerk. "Fine," I answered and walked out.

The long chance won!

"That man in the second floor front room is certainly 'a man of mystery.' I'd ask him to move if I didn't need the money so badly," said Mrs. Carsons, owner of a cheap rooming house, to Mrs. Murphy, a neighbor and friend.

"'A man of mystery'—what do you mean?" queried Mrs. Murphy.

"He gives his name as John Pashley, pays his rent regularly, and is always dressed well. He cooks all his meals, but," and here Mrs. Carsons had a tremor in her voice, "he gets no mail, has no visitors, does no work, and keeps the strangest hours. Sometimes he sleeps all day. He comes and goes in the wee hours of the morning. At times he doesn't leave the house for days, and occasionally he stays away altogether for two or three days. And the contents of his room—queer books; two framed pictures of a very beautiful girl; a scrap book of the most odd clippings from newspapers mostly about the different prisons in the country; and speaking of newspapers, he buys newspapers from Chicago, New York and Atlanta. He's been here three months now, yet he has not spoken to a soul in the house. So quiet, reserved and lonesome—he's hiding from something I bet—a very mysterious man."

As Mrs. Murphy was about to make some reply she was cut short by Mrs. Carsons. "Shush! Here he comes now. Look at him! You can't tell if he is twenty-five or forty. He looks both strong and weak—and do you notice that strange look in his eyes?"

And as the two women were scrutinizing "the man of mystery," I entered the house and went silently up to my room.

A man of mystery I was, with a price on my head, and a consuming fear in my heart. Lonesome, weary and hopeless—trying to lose myself in the city of Newark, N. J.

I did not have even the meagre satisfaction of corresponding with Lillian Salo. I had obtained her address from a friend in Chicago. I called her on the long distance phone and spoke to her. She agreed to come to New York if I would send her the money for her railroad fare. I sent it the next day, but she never arrived. Later the telegraph company returned the money saying they could not locate her. I never heard from her again.

On September 9, 1930, a short, dapper, heavily tanned man about 3 5 years old walked into the office of the *Newark Free Press*, on Academy St., Newark, N. J. He asked to see the advertising manager and emerged a member of the selling staff, engaged on a strictly commission basis. I had secured a position the second day I was in Newark.

The following afternoon I laid three orders for display space on the surprised manager's desk. A few moments later I received my commission check for $45.60. Not bad for a day's work. Here was a job worth holding.

Arriving at the office the next morning for a late edition before going to work, I received a great shock. The cause of this shock was another advertising salesman. I could not risk meeting this other salesman. This salesman had at one time worked on the *Chicago Evening Post,* and was well acquainted with me. I was not afraid of him—but I was sure he could not keep my secret to himself. No. I could not risk being identified.

In a few seconds I was back on the street, jobless again. The long arm of coincidence was reaching for me—reaching across thousands of miles and pointing its accusing finger at one out of millions.

There is the sting, the heartbreaking little things that make it so difficult for a fugitive to go straight and earn an honest living—always the shadow of the past blocking the road of the future, driving him unmercifully from job to job, from place to place.

One bright October morning in 1930 I walked into the National Labor Bank of Jersey City, N. J. I wished to open an account. "Right this way please," said a pleasant voice, and following, I found myself facing a snappy executive seated at a glass-topped desk. "What is your name, please?" inquired the executive. I winced, which was not observed by the banker. I wished now that I had not decided to open an account—but then, the banker could not surmise that I was an escaped convict.

Questions and answers. Every answer made by me was a fabrication. The ordeal was over at last. I laid down my money and received my passbook.

Building a new personality, gathering bit by bit identity cards, a bank book and other things so necessary to prove who you are, and in this case who you are not, the problems of an escaped convict are many and varied if he wants to go straight and take a normal place in the life of the community in which he resides.

What a surprise that bank executive would get if he knew that John Pashley was Robert E. Burns—the famous chain-gang fugitive.

I was standing at a street intersection, waiting for a car, in Journal Square, Jersey City. Another man was also standing there waiting. We looked intently at each other, and then the other man approached me, and spoke in a low voice.

"Say, aren't you Burns from Chicago?"

"Yes, hello, Hoffman."

"Well, by jove, Burns! I'm glad to see you. I read about your case in the papers, and I am glad to see that you got away. How are you getting along?"

"Pretty fair under the circumstances."

"That's fine. You certainly received a raw deal. Come on up to the house, the wife's away visiting her mother, so we'll have the house to ourselves."

Hoffman and I—two old cronies—meeting by accident—five years before we had been friends in Chicago. At that time I was struggling to create a civic magazine out of thin air, nerve and hard work; and George Hoffman was mastering the problems of civil engineering. We had belonged to the same club, but in the largeness of our efforts we had lost track of each other.

Five years have elapsed—a thousand miles are bridged and we meet in the fall of 1930—accidentally our paths cross among millions.

The police may require rest and sleep, but the long arm of coincidence is *always* at work; it never rests.

George Hoffman turned out to be a pleasant friend and a genial host. I had to relate my strange story over a fine dinner topped off with good cigars.

The subway was crowded when I got on at Forty-second Street and Broadway, New York. Habit, formed by constant vigilance, caused me to study every face in the car. Always on the lookout for the face of the enemy—for some person who might be ready to reach out and put an end to my freedom.

And there to my amazement was Kier!

George Kier, a professional subscription solicitor for magazines. He had at one time been employed by me in Chicago as the circulation manager of the *Greater Chicago Magazine*.

He also recognized me instantly. Placing a finger on my lips as a sign of silence to him, I edged through the crowded car to his side.

"Hello, Kier."

"Hello, Mr. Williams." (This was Kier's invention for my protection, not knowing what name I was using). We discussed old friends, bygone days, and my case.

Kier was much impressed by the fact that I had escaped the second time, and he was emphatic in saying that I had received a bum deal.

My!—it gave me a great kick to meet some one from Chicago with whom I was closely acquainted. Here was a man who for three years had worked with me and had helped me to build *The Greater Chicago Magazine*. We enjoyed a pleasant evening talking over old times.

Again the long arm of coincidence proved that it is *always* on the job—mixing the past with the present—bridging the gap of great distances. Some day, perhaps, it will reach into the past and bring out of its magic bag the wrong man. Then my freedom may end.

It was 10 o'clock at night, April 1, 1931, and a slow drizzle was falling. Slinking forms were darting in and out of doorways to escape the rain. Here and there a light vainly tried to shine through the rain and mist casting fleeting shadows up and down the almost deserted street.

I walked along the street towards the Newark Y. M. C. A. I was thinking about the vagaries of the "long arm of coincidence." Being a fugitive I felt some intangible danger or some unexpected occurrence. Something was about to happen. I looked about in every direction like a startled deer—sniffing the air for clues, as it were, and then!—I was face to face with another man!

Could it be he? Impossible! And yet—into his eyes came a faint flicker of recognition. I passed him by, it just could not be he. Five steps past, and, impelled by an incredulous brain, I retraced my steps.

Again we are face to face, our eyes talking, studying, appraising, questioning. Our senses refused for a moment to accept cold facts. Mutual doubt was dispelled at last. We shake hands, and speak as one.

"Hello, Burns."

"Hello, Moore."

"Moore, this is unbelievable," I said, after a brief pause.

"Burns, it's almost nine years since we last saw each other, and then we were both in the chain gang."

"Yes, and when we first met in Atlanta in March, 1922, it was raining just as it is now. We parted in the Fulton County chain gang in April, 1922—nine years, almost to the day."

"I read your story and everybody is commenting on it. It is about time someone exposed the frightful conditions down there. But this is a preposterous coincidence. No one would ever believe it."

The long arm of coincidence! No fiction writer would ever dare to imagine what actually happened on April 1, 1931, in Newark, N. J.

Let's examine the threads of destiny that wove the texture of our thoughts and lives, and made us fugitives together.

John Moore and I were broke and hungry. We met by accident in the city of Atlanta on a rainy night in March, 1922. The following day, acting under the spell and direction of a third man, Sidney Flagg, we took part in a $5.80 robbery. We were caught and sentenced to the chain gang. Flagg received thirty to forty years; Moore eight to twelve; and I, six to ten years.

John Moore also escaped from the chain gang in September, 1924. Neither of us had seen nor heard of the other since I was transferred from the Fulton County chain gang in April, 1922.

We became two fugitives wandering from place to place, dodging the arm of the law. In all of the immense territory of the forty-eight states, thousands of cities, and one hundred twenty-six million people, and with the police of the nation searching for us both, our paths crossed at the same spot, at the same time—10 P.M., April 1, 1931—at Warren and Halsey Streets, Newark, N. J.

The arm of the law may be long—but the arm of coincidence is longer—it performs the impossible!

On the same kind of rainy night—and in the same condition—broke, friendless and weary—we met again. Two fugitives—facing with fear and dread the nightmare and horrors of the chain gang.

Neither of us would ever think of committing such a crime again. We have learned a bitter lesson. We have become honest, law-abiding citizens. We are striving against tremendous odds. Can we win?

Blocking our paths stands the chilly iron statue of blind justice, resting on the rock of tradition. What human power can thaw just a little this iron lady so that the milk of human kindness may flow through her breast? What human power can set her cold heart beating with the warmth of human mercy and understanding? Through all the ages her numberless victims have cried in vain, their pleas unheard by iron ears, their sufferings unseen by sightless eyes. How long will justice based on tradition mock at man?

"Gee whiz, Burns, what a kick the Georgia authorities would get if they could grab us both now? How overjoyed they would be," said Moore, speaking as much to himself as to me.

"Moore, don't ever get in trouble again—obey the law at all times, no matter how unreasonable it may seem, and perhaps some day we can make the authorities down there see how ridiculous their desire to punish us further really is," I replied.

"You described conditions very accurately, but words do not convey the horror, the brutality, the uselessness of the chain gang. No one can imagine what it is really like unless he has been there," Moore continued.

"It's now my life's ambition to destroy the chain-gang system in Georgia, and see substituted in its place a more humane and enlightened system of correction," I answered.

Space will not permit all the conversation that passed between us. One thing is certain. Georgia is not satisfied that we in our long years of freedom are leading honest and useful lives.

Conditionally pardoning or paroling Moore and me would be but a simple act of mercy and human understanding. The cause of justice would in no wise suffer— in fact, enlightened justice implies that where the culprit *has* repented and reformed, punishment is no longer necessary. The original purpose of the punishment was correction—now that correction has taken place, why continue the punishment?

We finally separated to go our respective ways. With a hearty handshake and a common knowledge of our common danger, we melted away into the misty shadows of the dismal night.

Seeking a position in these times of depression is wearisome. There are thirty applicants for every job. Most of these applicants are armed with sterling references of their past performances. What chance has an escaped convict, who has to give a fictitious name, has no references and whose past must be manufactured in the questionable realm of his imagination?

Walking into an employment agency, the first thing I met was an application. "Please fill out this application, so we shall be better able to help you secure a position," said a voice at the desk, handing me an application blank.

I read it over. There were the usual stereotyped questions: name, age, married or single, address, etc. Reading further I discovered that there were spaces for my entire past career. Did you ever attempt to fill out such a record of your life from imagination—create out of nothing a past to fit the present? It is quite a mental trick. Then in a few days or a week later try to remember what you wrote on that application!

I filled out a dozen applications in an equal number of places, each one different. Later, in calling back, I discovered that I could not remember what I had written on each one. It made me dizzy trying to memorize the fictitious past performances of the mythical personage John Pashley I was trying to create.

I gave up. It was useless to try to find a place in society to which my ability and intelligence entitled me. The alternative was to lose myself in some menial, unimportant occupation usually filled by drifters or defeated individuals like myself. Dishwasher, waiter, counterman or porter, take your choice.

Beaten! Not through lack of intelligence, desire or effort, but beaten by the fact that I was a fugitive.

On February 28, 1931, the fifty-percent veteran's loan act was passed by Congress. My brother had previously secured a twenty-percent loan on my soldier's bonus to finance my mother's trips to Georgia. Under the new law I could secure an additional loan of $481.00. I needed this money as I was planning to start a small business.

In order to make this additional loan it would be necessary for me to go personally to the loan office in Newark, N. J., and fill out the required papers. I would have to appear there as Robert E. Burns and go through all the red tape usual to such applications.

Could I, an escaped convict, not yet six months out of prison, afford to take such a chance?

I had my heart set on a business I wanted to establish and I needed the money badly. Still it was far better to be free and broke. There was great risk of detection involved, for it was certainly possible that the Department of Justice in Washington would have notified the director of the Newark district to be on the lookout for me, as my brother had made the first loan there, and the original certificate was in the Newark files.

After several days of thought and worry I fell back on my old standby—"Courage has magic, power and genius in it."

Boldly I walked into the office of the Veteran's Bureau in Newark on Bleeker Street near Halsey. Right across the way was a famous speakeasy.

Inside the Veteran's Bureau was a long wooden counter serviced by half a dozen clerks. Finally it came my turn, and addressing me, the clerk said:

"What's your name?"

Just as I was about to answer I noticed a policeman in full uniform standing right beside me. For an instant I was speechless. Fear gripped my heart with icy talons. It was March, and the third number of my story was on all the news-stands. Was he up on all the circulars sent to his station regarding wanted men? Surely I was a fool to expect to get away with this!

But the die was cast.

"Robert E. Burns," I answered.

The name made no impression on the policeman or the clerk or those nearby, and in a few moments I was back on the street much relieved. I gave my address care of my brother in Palisade, N. J., to which the check was finally sent.

Upon receiving the money I started the "National Retail Sales Builders," located at 60 Warren Street, Newark.

The idea and purpose of this business was to stimulate retail sales in community stores. The retailer subscribing to this service received six pairs of silk stockings, two window displays, one thousand circulars explaining the plan in detail and five hundred come-back cards and a nickel-plated punch. Each of the cards contained amounts of from five cents to twenty-five cents and the full amount totaled ten dollars. When a customer entered and purchased say eighty cents worth of merchandise he or she received a come-back card which was punched in the amount purchased. The customer was to keep the card and whenever he or she made additional purchases they brought the card with them and had it punched for the amount spent. When the card was all punched, which indicated that that particular customer had spent $10 in that store, he or she received a pair of the silk stockings.

The plan was on the old trading-stamp idea and was to be an inducement for housewives to buy from their local stores.

All the literature bore the individual retailer's name, address and advertising and really appeared as a personal effort of his own.

To start this business, which to me seemed sure of success, required art work, engraving, etc., for the window displays, and considerable outlay in printing, silk stockings, punches, etc.

When all was set I worked hard and faithfully and secured a few orders—each order cost the retailer complete $10. However, when I attempted to collect for the service, I was up against a stone wall. Every independent retailer was broke or almost so and could only pay on the installment plan.

I purchased the stockings direct from a mill in Paterson—and they were high grade seconds—yet they were never accepted by stores operated by women.

After two months of strife and struggle and strenuous sales effort I was still in business but broke.

Also about this time I heard that a Department of Justice agent from Washington was in the vicinity trying to pick up my trail, so it was move again—constantly drifting from place to place—one jump ahead of my pursuers. The month of May, 1931, found me moving, jobless and broke again—the business and investment left by the wayside.

I feel sure that if I had had my freedom I would have eventually made a success of that business, but trying to build a business and dodge the law at the same time is too much for any man.

At the cost of five dollars in a labor agency, I secured a job as laborer on a road job near Ridgewood, N. J., at four dollars a day, where at the moment I am writing this, on the first anniversary of my second escape, September 4, 1931.

I am sitting in my plainly furnished cheap room, alone, writing this record of events with hands horny from heavy toil. I am now John Pashley—an itinerant laborer—friendless—weary of body and mind—only my heart after years of tragic events beats bravely on—hoping against hope that some day its sturdy beats will eventually hammer out a place for me somewhere—somehow—some time.

On a beautiful Sunday afternoon in the year 1931 three persons are standing beside a peaceful grave in Kensico cemetery in New York. There, slumbering in the quiet earth lies a beloved husband and a dutiful and loving father. It is the grave of James H. Burns, a godly and honest man.

In the beauty and the glory of God's loving presence three heads are bowed in silent prayer. Mrs. Katherine Burns—loving wife and mother; her two sons, Rev. Vincent G. Burns, a prominent minister of Jesus' sacred promise, and I, Robert E. Burns, branded with the mark of escaped convict—stand side by side.

Mother, minister and fugitive, paying silent tribute to the memory of a dear one who has passed on.

A fugitive beside my father's grave! Was I a desperate enemy of society, whose presence outside of prison walls was a menace to the peace of the world? How ridiculous! Today I am *not* a criminal, my sole ambition is to become a useful member of society. But the law does not recognize that I have changed—is not even concerned with my reformation—the law merely demands its pound of flesh.

In a sane, intelligent and loving society, justice would be wide-awake and ready to help those who by virtue of their environment have become mentally and spiritually sick. Simple justice should be happy when the weak one has become strong again—and should say as the Master said, "Go—and sin no more." *That* was the Son of God's command; *that* is the very essence of justice.

But that would not satisfy the chain-gang system of Georgia. Theirs is a different code. Born and raised in the atmosphere of slavery, life is cheap and of little value. There, framed in the natural beauty of God's handiwork, still survives an ancient tradition—revenge! The very word echoes and re-echoes through the beautiful pines and mountain tops of the State of Georgia. Feuds, lynchings, intolerance, illiteracy and hatred have survived through that one word—revenge!

"Mr. Burns will certainly get first-hand information about sleeping in chains if he is ever my guest again," said Warden Hardy in the *Atlanta Journal.*

Is this expression befitting a warden whose duty it is to help reform and train men for a useful place in society?

Perhaps I am wrong. Perhaps men and women are sent to prison solely for brutal punishment, and a warden's duty is to inflict that punishment—and then let the helpless convict leave the prison with a scar on his heart—a tortured brain—and a hope forever gone. What do you think?